Two Winters in a Tipi

Two Winters in a Tipi

My Search for the Soul of the Forest

Mark Warren

LYONS PRESS
Guilford, Connecticut
An imprint of Globe Pequot Press

Lyons Press is an imprint of Globe Pequot Press

Project editor: Ellen Urban
Layout artist: Justin Marciano

Library of Congress Cataloging-in-Publication Data

Warren, Mark, 1947-
Two winters in a tipi : my search for the soul of the forest / Mark
Warren.
p. cm.
ISBN 978-0-7627-7922-2
1. Tipis—History. 2. Tipis—Design and constructions. I. Title.
E98.D9W26 2012
796.54028'4—dc23
2012000143

Printed in the United States of America

10 9 8 7 6 5 4 3 2 1

For Elly,
just across the river

Contents

Prologue

One moonless night during my tipi years, I slipped from my bedding, dressed, and stepped out into the cold. I often did this simply to stand under the stars and listen to the nocturnal sounds coming from the forest bordering the meadow. Clicks, chirrs, and wing flaps marked the pulse of nature's business hours, and I loved nothing more than to audit the flow of nightlife, to feel connected to it if only peripherally.

I had practiced this same vigil when I lived in a house, but back then it wasn't a nightly habit. When I did stand on my porch in the wee hours, I was fully aware of how much was going on out there in the shadows, but I knew it then as something separate from my life. Ultimately I would turn my back and return to oblivious sleep in a soft bed surrounded by insulated walls, drawn curtains, and evenly distributed heat. Though a tipi is wonderfully snug, private, and sheltering, a thin line divides outside from inside. Once you step out, you realize that there really has been no transition; you were already a part of the surroundings.

Far down the length of the field, against the lighter shade of starlit grass, eight dark shapes clustered together on a rise. They stood still as boulders. After a few minutes, two of the amorphous shapes drifted apart in slow and silent movements, giving the appearance of black buoys floating on pale, luminescent water. The movement marked them as nocturnal foragers: a herd of deer browsing the succulent new shoots of early spring. It was a scene so pastoral, serene, and otherworldly that it struck me as an invitation; I wanted to be a part of that picture.

For more than an hour, I stalked low in the tall winter-killed grasses as I made my way toward the rise. I moved with patience and fluidity, eventually on hands and knees, and then on my belly. The previous season's dead grasses stood two feet high, wan and brittle, providing cover. The wind was blowing gently toward me, carrying my scent away from the deer. The desiccated grass vibrated with a sustained whisper of tapping leaves and stems, like paper-thin blades trying to sharpen themselves against one another.

Just a few yards from the herd, I slowly raised my head, settled in, and watched them graze. Their profiles were crisply defined. Their heads bobbed down, and when they came up, I could see and hear their jaws grinding laterally as their dark eyes held a steady vigil on the borders of the field. The constant edge of alertness on which they lived was palpable.

Then one of the animals fixed its stare on me—and stiffened. Every fiber of its being seemed focused on identifying what I was. There was no stamping of hoof, no snort, no sudden burst of alarm, or dash to escape. The other deer seemed not to notice our silent standoff. Then the vigilant deer stepped away, the others following as if the herd were interconnected by a single delicate thread. Without consciously deciding to do so, I rose to a crouch and flowed with them, deer-like, bent forward at the waist, my torso horizontal.

Still, they didn't bolt. They moved deliberately but without panic, and I was perfectly able to keep up. They were allowing me a moment in the brotherhood of the wilderness. Soon their gliding bodies picked up speed by increments, testing my capabilities, until I was running upright, strong and effortless, fueled by the brisk night air. I was not chasing them but running with them, inside the herd. Quickly veering to either side, I could have touched one's flank. But I didn't. I wanted to do exactly what they were doing. To stretch out my stride with God-given grace. To feel the freedom of flying through the night grass. I had come to be with them—now I was *of* them.

A boundless energy filled me with preternatural strength, making me feel light and fleet, gathered against gravity as my feet seemed hardly to touch the ground. The wind blew in my face, making a hollow whisper in my ears that masked all other sounds and gave the experience a surreal, dreamlike quality.

We ran like this for sixty yards, together, choreographed by some tacit agreement granted by divine intervention, serendipity, or perhaps the generosity of deer. The night expanded—like that so-called flash of life in the compressed seconds before death. The stars fixed the moment in place with a thousand distant flashbulbs that ensured my detailed memory of the night.

That was nearly thirty years ago. These days, I don't sleep so close to that edge of possibility, nor am I as fleet of foot. More important, insulated walls sequester me, layers of material separate me from the earth, and the vigilance of a thermostat incubates me. As with other men's castles, an abstraction of the moat that encircles it greatly defines mine.

All my life I have paid attention to nature. I followed it as though it were a phantom figure slinking off into the woods, and I *had* to track it, to know what it was. Such was *my* nature, which led me through a gamut of adventures, both grand and minute: calling in more than a hundred raucous crows to wheel at treetop level above my hiding place for a half hour as they screamed a chorus of complaint over my newly perfected raven croak; discovering the wildly intoxicating flood of scent exuded from a red-spotted millipede or a crushed black snakeroot seed; walking under the dark mystery of hemlocks while the fold and foam of mountain water manufactured a liquid white light from within; stalking and observing the secret lives of bear and fox, vole and cricket.

I had moved closer to nature with every day of my life. I was, after all, a naturalist, whose life mission was to learn as much as I could about the wild things so that I could teach others. Learning is my passion. Perhaps teaching has served as a justification for the learning. I didn't realize just how much moving into a tipi would accelerate my learning experiences. But catapult me forward it did, like the night I ran with the deer.

My rate of education soared, paradoxically, by slowing down my life to a wonderfully inclusive series of rhythms such as the unhurried but deliberate ascent of the moon, the quiet passing of a raccoon that came to me one night to die, the long stalk across the meadow that allowed me to rise up among deer and run wild. These events cannot be corner-cut or compressed to suit any agenda other than what is real and natural. To witness them, you must release yourself from time. That was the tipi's gift to me, that temporal liberation. Once you've grasped it, there is no letting go.

In tipi-life, there is always work to do: wood to cut, laundry to knead at the creek, drinking water to haul, pots to scour with sand and pebbles, and food to gather and prepare. You might think that I had to hurry to fit everything in during daylight hours—but that didn't happen. A new and natural pace took hold: Everything slowed. As it did, my education exploded in a sunburst of directions simply because I was never separated from nature. If a tree fell in the forest, as the saying goes, I was there to hear it.

Before the tipi, I might explore and stay out all day, even a week; but always I returned to where I had started: my house. Home is the magnet that draws us back. It is the place where we are deeply, subconsciously connected to our version of normalcy, dependency, and complacency. Home is always waiting with its pantry of foods, its medicine cabinet of remedies, its faucets of thirst-quenching refreshment, its nurturing nest of mattress, pillow, and cool cotton sheets.

Even on my self-imposed survival trips—adventures that my soul craved each season—home always waited at the end to counterbalance any temporary discomfort that might have poked an elbow into the experience. Home is where I went to recover. Home is our physical safety net.

A tipi is most certainly a home. In fact, it is a grand place to live. But leaning down to step from the oval doorway into the boundless world of nature is not like walking out the back door of your home. That single step from the tipi is no departure at all. The ground is the same. But the step is profoundly personal, exposing you to the watchful eyes of the wild. Even before you leave the tipi, you are connected to the outer world around you in ways that make the old Plains Indian lodging not an encapsulated retreat from nature but an integral part of it.

There are physical explanations for this. For one thing, a tipi cover is intentionally raised several inches off the ground, leaving a gap for the influx of air. This same gap, of course, invites a parade of curious mice . . . and insects . . . and snakes . . . and just about anything else small enough to make the squeeze.

The walls are thin. You can hear everything out there. But there is a mystery to it. The conical shape of the tipi swirls sound in a disorienting way, so that it's hard to pinpoint the direction from which a sound originates.

Rain thrums on the canvas just inches from your sleeping place. The sound is not muted and removed like the distant drumming upon a shingled roof; it is immediate, intimate, and soporific. As they are meant to, raindrops run down the long poles inside the tipi all the way to the ground. So there is an alliance with rain. It can come inside, but it must adhere to the rules.

The backbone of any tipi is its fanned-out cone of trimmed trees leaning together into a common juncture, making a near circular floor plan at ground level. In one of the pie-sections of my floor, I stacked small, broken limbs of wood for fast-lighting fuel. Fire and smoke are living parts of tipi-life. Architecturally mandated big, heavy reflector stones ringed the fire pit. Beneath my summer bedding lay a protective barrier of pawpaw, hickory, and sassafras leaves—all to ward off siege by chiggers. Wrens and phoebes regularly flitted inside to investigate, no doubt considering a nesting site, until the evening fire and billowing smoke announced that all bets were off.

By sight and scent, these interior features reflect more the essence of a forest than a living room. The tipi—unlike angular homes—is less about separation than integration. It rests lightly upon the land. Whenever I packed one up and moved on, the land soon showed no sign of tenancy. But while I was there, I lived close to the earth. Scents and sounds and silences wafted through the cover as easily as smoke rose from the tipi's smoke hole. The stars kept watch through that same opening. Perhaps it was they who whispered to me that night. *Get up! The deer are waiting for you in the meadow.*

In the forest my natural inclination has always been to move slowly, quietly. But inside all my previous homes, I had been less attentive to my own movement. We accept the thump of our shoes on floorboards and rugs, and we move at a speed dictated by a given day's agenda and the clock that rules from the bedside table, the wrist, or the pocket. The reassuring sights and sounds of "life-support" surround us in houses: the late-night light inside the humming refrigerator, the whir of a fan, the flush of a toilet.

That night in the meadow with the dark ghosts of deer silently leaping beside me, I ran as I had never run in track or football or any childhood game. With the deer, I ran like the wind. But there is an irony. The clocks of the world broke that night, and the event transformed itself from a primal urge for speed to the slow and limitless expansion of an unforgettable moment. The entire experience was born of my tipi-life because stepping over the tipi's threshold to enter that night required no adjustment. Sleeping inside the tipi, I was already a part of the night.

The deer and I ran together all the way to the edge of the meadow where, without urgency or panic, they fanned out, slipped without a sound into the great shadow of forest, and then dissolved, black into black, like magicians leaping through hidden mirrors.

Suddenly alone, I stood beneath the night sky breathing deeply, though not winded. The air was delicious. I was forty-two years old, and I could have run all night—but not in the forest. For that I would have needed nocturnal eyes. The night air touched my moist skin with the coolness of mountain water. Behind me the meadow took on the aura of hallowed ground. I was changed, enriched.

Metaphorically, I had run like the wind before. I had achieved this same Aeolian experience when closing a cherished book, loosing a first arrow from a homemade bow, or conjuring a flame by spinning dead wood in my hands. And I have known this burst of freedom in the simplicity of honest words shared with a friend. I have also known it in silence. But this was the first time I had elevated the simile to its literal meaning by running with the deer.

That unforgettable sixty-yard sprint traced back to tipi-life, just as the first flight of a fledgling hawk is made grand by virtue of its nest perched high in a lofty pine. There are no mediocre excursions. Furthermore, coming home to a tipi does not mean leaving the pulse and flow of the natural world. In a sense, no matter where you are in the forest, you are always at home. The tipi simply covers the patch of that home where you have chosen to sleep.

Later that night, nestled back into my bedding, I listened to a screech owl whistle its eerie, descending tremolo. I knew the deer heard it, too. We were all connected. I had always known that in my head. Now that I had run with them on a cool spring night in a mountain meadow, I carried proof of it in the warmth of my blood.

Trial by Fire

In 1989, a midnight August storm unleashed a bolt of fire, connecting heaven and earth through the mountain farmhouse in which I had been living for the past seven years. Crude columns of hand-stacked stones propped the old wood-frame building, built almost a century earlier, two feet above the ground. Its sagging interior wood flooring had at some point been covered with creaking linoleum, its roof nailed with tin. That roof, the fire investigator later told me, reflected heat downward like an oven, turning the fire into a blistering inferno. Nothing survived it, not even metal tools.

Everything I owned was incinerated in an un-stoppable blaze that must have lit up the driving rain like falling diamonds. I don't know because I didn't see it. My dog, Elly, and I were fifty miles away, sleeping at the summer camp where I had just returned campers after a week-long wilderness program on this same leased mountain land.

The call came the next morning. I was packing gear and about to return home when one of the camp owners came out of the office and called me to the phone. She followed me back inside. A woman not given to shows of emotion, she put her arms around my chest as though to hold me in place when I picked up the phone. Then the side of her face pressed into my back.

Through the line, I barely recognized Teresa, my closest friend in the mountains. Her voice sounded small, squeezed from an unfamiliar place. She asked about me and how I was doing, but a vacuum pulled at the core of her sentences. She was trying to prepare me.

"Last night there was a bad storm," she said finally. "Lots of lightning." Then after a pause, her voice resigned to a forced, even timbre. "Your house burned down."

The hum on the telephone line dropped away. Her soft words had delivered a slap of finality that sucked up all the electricity in the wire.

"Oh," I said.

My voice sounded muted and distant, as though I were hearing myself from underwater. The camp owner's grip tightened around my chest.

Teresa wanted to know if she could do anything, but what was there to do? I thanked her for calling, hung up the phone, and extricated myself from my unexpected support system with an attempt at a grateful smile, insisting that I was okay.

"I need to go home," I said.

She nodded, and her expression said, *Of course*; though, when I thought about it, I wasn't sure why I had to go. There was no home to go to, nothing to do there. Some things, however, need to be seen before they can be real to you.

Walking outside into the sunlight. I felt quiet—and alive. *What if Elly and I had been in the house last night?*

Elly, as usual, was waiting for me in the cool shade of the bushes just outside the office. At the bang of the screened door and the familiar rhythm of my footsteps, she sprang up at a fast walk at my side to be sure she wasn't forgotten. Together we marched to my truck, and as soon as I opened the door, she jumped in. Before starting the engine I looked at her. What might she sense from me on this landmark of a day?

The previous afternoon, I had dropped off my camping gear before leaving home. All of it was gone now. Minor things came to mind—sleeping bag, tent, mess kit . . . but these were the first lost items to register.

"Well," I said, looking around the cab, "I've got the truck . . . my guitar . . ." I laid my hand on a stack of field guides. "These books . . . a raincoat . . ." I looked down at myself appraisingly, as if someone else had dressed me that morning. "These clothes . . ." I patted the leather sheath on my belt. "My knife."

Elly had been watching me throughout my monologue. "And you," I whispered. Her body made a subtle tremor, as if a wag had originated in her brain but fizzled before reaching her tail.

Elly was always with me. What if she had been a housedog, and I had left her at home yesterday when I brought my campers back? Therein lay the silver lining to this violent cloud. I reached over and stroked her head. She looked out the front windshield and shifted her weight on her front paws. Then she gave me that look that said, *Let's get this thing going. I want to get home.*

Home.

Even the word was forcing upon us a new definition. It had become a loose and immeasurable sphere that surrounded us, an invisible bubble of air, pliable enough to fit any space I chose. Where we went, it went.

Driving down the highway, I began to understand that what I had inventoried inside the truck really *was* the sum total of what I claimed on this earth. Elly, who looked back at me as she always had, knew a lot more about all this than I did. Possessions . . . or the lack thereof. What was important? What wasn't? She had already grasped this on the most fundamental level. The highway spooled out before us, and I realized that I was just now catching up to her way of thinking.

Smoke lifted lazily into the air as we pulled up to the charred ruins of the house. It shredded through the blackened limbs of the scorched sycamore and oak that had shaded the front porch. But for the absurdity of the concrete front steps standing alone above the ash like a pulpit, there was nothing left to remind me of a house. Even the tin roof had vanished.

Acrid air bit our noses with irreverent odors never intended for release, heat still radiating from the debris like the foul breath of a gluttonous monster that had eaten itself into a stupor. No sound but the faint tick, pop, sizzle of settling embers.

Elly jumped from her seat onto the scorched grass and walked over to the place in front of the steps where it was her habit to keep guard in the shade of the sycamore. Now, with the leaves burned away, the great summer shadow she had known was mottled and web-like—little more than the streaking of winter's bare limbs. She dropped down on her belly, face toward the road, paying no attention to the pile of smoldering rubble where the house had been.

I walked the perimeter of the blackened foundation, mesmerized by the open space that had appeared. Sunlight swept uninterrupted through new territory, a volume of air where even light had been denied for a century.

When you lose everything at once like this, there is no way to fathom the sum of the losses. The process is an unbelievably long itemization of "stuff" that trickles back to memory in scattered bits. I imagine that this is a protective safeguard for the spirit, like shock. Something comes to mind thirteen years later, and you let out a whimsical snort at not having thought of it before. *How important could that have been?*

My house had been like a small nature center, and the students who had come to this land for workshops always enjoyed browsing its walls and shelves. Sometimes, when I ran into summer campers years after their time with me, they reminisced over fellow campers and our exploits. They always mentioned the treasures that had adorned my walls: antlers, skulls, pouches made of tanned skins, pelts with exquisite hair, bones, feathers, claws, cast tracks, beaver gnawings, homemade bows and arrows, quivers, moccasins, drums, deerskin clothing, lacrosse sticks, spears, arrowheads, atlatl, and a collection of driftwood that revealed a canoeist's case of borderline kleptomania.

Standing there by the ruin of my home, I felt no need to assess the value of these possessions. Neither my landlord nor I had insurance. Losing those things seemed a part of some natural order, an unspoken law; they had gone back to a place from which they had come. One mound of the ruins, however, continued to draw my attention.

This last pile of coals glowed orange-red, the heat visibly intense, rippling the air above it and distorting the trees beyond. This "last stand" against the inferno had been my piano—and on the piano, I realized with a catch in my throat, I had laid the novel I had been writing for the last seven years, my first attempt at a full-length book. Then, unable to pull my eyes away as my mind reeled, I remembered that beneath the manuscript lay five composition books filled with the music I had written over the last three-quarters of my life. These scribblings—little etch-marks on paper—became the most salient losses of the fire.

My gain, I later came to understand, was learning that contradiction—as quietly immutable as it is beside logic—hovers around us all the time. It is only in a powerful, shifted moment like this perhaps, when everything goes up in flames, that we get a glimpse of it. The contradiction gave me choices, the themes of which were as diametric as the two ends of the same arrow.

Limitations imprisoned me. Denied my former gamut of options, I couldn't, for instance, take off in my canoe and disappear for a few days. My canoe had become a glob of melted plastic.

Or I could declare myself liberated. There was nothing to take care of. If I wanted to take off for a month, there were no arrangements to make for paying the electric bill, no food spoiling in the refrigerator, no calls to return.

The weight of the tragedy felt immense. I wasn't sure how I would crawl out from under it. Yet, I was light, like a migrating bird wheeling on the wind, with the new freedom to set my course wherever I desired. I was homeless . . . and yet I was more grounded than ever before.

I had a decision to make. I'd been living on leased land as a temporary base for my nature and survival programs until I could find the right piece of land to buy. Holding the deed to the perfect mountain property had been my lifelong dream, and my current home had given me a tantalizing taste of that dream. It would be hard to leave this acreage, true, with its varied topography, its streams, peaks and valleys, woods and meadows, for another interim property. If I moved, I wanted it to be the last time, onto that coveted ground that was to be my permanent territory.

I had money. I had been living the life of the poor in order to save all the paychecks from my adult life. In every abode I had rented for the past twenty-five years, the financial arrangement had included some measure of barter, trading a portion or all of the rent in exchange for labor. I lived as if my savings did not exist. That money was for the land and nothing else.

Now, without a house to afford me shelter, my landlord dropped my rent to zero. Serving as caretaker of the land, he said, was barter enough for my staying on the grounds. So stay I did—at least until I bought my own homeland.

Ben and Dana, Teresa's best friends and patron saints of the scorched and roofless, lent me a tent that I set up in the most remote corner of the back meadow. This was deeper into the property, well beyond earshot of the road, which dead-ended at the house. My new site, high on a ridge, overlooked the Etowah River. All day and night I could hear the rapids, like an endless sigh exhaling from deep in the valley.

The tent provided a spare living space with a simplicity that suited me. Each time I unzipped the door to enter, I could count my belongings on one hand. Blanket, guitar, books, water bottle, and a cardboard box of assorted foods. Elly declined use of the tent and slept outside.

After a month, the tent fly ripped, brittle as charred gauze. UV rays beating down day after day had desiccated the nylon. A piece of plastic from the roadside easily replaced it, but the remedy was only temporary. This was my second eviction notice delivered by celestial fire. Fall was on its way, and then winter. I didn't want to fend against the cold by wrapping up inside a cocoon of blankets. I wanted to do things in my home at night—carve, sew, read, write, play music.

That afternoon as Elly and I dragged firewood from the forest, I took a new perspective on the dome tent, which now seemed squat and a little forlorn . . . like all tents are when you leave them up too long in one place. Tents, by nature of their compactness and mobility, suggest moving on—which I didn't want to do right now.

The fire ring several yards from the tent appeared disconnected and illogical, as if inanely intended to warm up the entire atmosphere. I was immediately dissatisfied. The tent, with its ragged makeshift cap, looked destitute. In its place I visualized something tall, braced by sturdy wood. I imagined a fire inside and living spaces delineated like the slices of a pie.

"I should be living in a tipi," I thought. Elly gave me a curious look, and I realized I had spoken aloud.

My words spilled out onto the wind and drifted down into the swale of the meadow like a carrier pigeon striking out on a mission of vital importance. My inner compass suddenly shifted, pointing to a new angle bright with promise. Excitement stirred within my chest.

The next morning I started looking into tipis.

~ 2 ~

Native Son

When I opened my eyes the next morning, the tipi idea was still hovering beside me, like a child at dawn on Christmas morning eagerly waiting for me to wake up. It was too early to make calls, so I went about my usual morning camp chores: building a fire, fixing breakfast, washing up at the river. After that, there were still another two hours before businesses would open, so I returned to my bedding and stretched out to think about my new choice of abode.

It could never be called a stretch for me, this idea of living in a tipi. The Native Americans had served as my perfect mentors for a long time. I had, after all, begun my life smack in the heart of their tribal homeland. Historically, eastern tribes hadn't used tipis. They had no need for a breakdown tent. The woodland people here didn't need to follow migrating herds of animals because the vast and diversified forest—from the Mississippi River to the Atlantic—provided a year-round paradise for most creatures. If hunting overkilled a section of forest, the vacuum soon filled like water obeying the law of gravity. Expanding populations of animal species see emptiness as opportunity.

The Muskogee had once walked the sylvan trails in the piedmont forests of my childhood, and just north of me, where I was to live in the mountains, the Cherokee. All of Georgia had been the "property" of these native people, though they wouldn't have phrased it that way. They honored boundaries for the sake of clarity and intertribal equilibrium. For the most part, native tribes did not embrace the concept of owning parts of the earth, at least not until Europeans forced the abstraction—and the paperwork—on them. Such an idea of ownership was presumptuous and disrespectful to the Maker of All Things. As one famous northwestern chief once put it, one might as well claim ownership of the air.

Though mutual enemies, the Cherokee and the Muskogee developed cultures that overlapped with many similarities. And why not? They shared the most common of denominators: the land. Environment shapes cultures like nothing else—or at least it used to.

In our time it might not be so easy to fathom how land shapes people. Too many artificial variables are thrown into the equation. Long ago, a man, spear in hand, chased elk through the mountains on a regular basis and surely developed a stalwart physique. Everything about his rugged appearance would have reflected his excellence in the hunt.

Today a pale and pudgy scion of any paleo-man can effortlessly surpass his ancestor's abilities to reach that same goal of putting food in his stomach. Twist the key, step on the accelerator, drive to the grocery store, and browse the meat section where a sundry herd of critters obediently awaits the hunter without his even pulling back a bowstring. He takes his prize home, sticks it in the oven, turns a dial, and puts his feet up for an hour as he tests his acuity against the contestants on *Wheel of Fortune.*

His is the modern high-tech equation that we now think of as the norm. Both paths leave imprints on the user and upon the earth, but they contain vastly disparate sets of tracks. Neither man could trade places with the other and succeed. Early man couldn't know how to operate a car. Conversely, modern man couldn't keep up with the elk. But the paleo-man could reject the automobile, head to the hills, fashion a weapon, and resort to his tried-and-true method of the hunt. The modern man, if placed in the paleo-man's time, could not reciprocate. He hasn't the luxury of eschewing the primitive, predatory sprint to wait thousands of years for the advent of the internal combustion engine.

The Cherokee were a mountain people. The Muskogee spread from the piedmont into the coastal plain. There were and are unique differences to these geographic areas, but because they were contiguous, the piedmont Muskogee and the montane Cherokee shared a botanical and geological overlap in their environments. Both lived in the Great Eastern Woodlands, which still cover the eastern third of America, albeit in ever-diminishing islands of green.

By virtue of its thick cover and leafy carpet, these Eastern Woodlands made extraordinary stalkers of its first people. Highly advanced long-distance weaponry didn't work effectively in a hunting ground so cluttered with deflecting objects: shrubs, vines, tree trunks, branches, and leaves. The supreme and necessary tool was stealth . . . to close the distance between hunter and prey for a clean, unobstructed shot.

These people learned the skill of stalking from the same local master stalkers who predated them: cougar, wolf, fox, heron, and a host of others. Even prey animals like deer know how to stalk—in their case, away from danger. All these animals became the unwitting teachers, as the humans observed, adopted, and adapted the wild techniques as their own.

A little more than a century after these people were purged from their land, along came a young boy tracing the same paths across the same terrain, encountering the same rocks, plants, animals, and creeks. What better place to turn for guidance, illumination, and camaraderie than these natives who knew the forest as no people have since. The Cherokee and the Muskogee learned the forest out of utilitarian necessity. Because of their conscious dependency upon trees, stone, herbs, animals, creeks, and so on, they never lost their hold on reverential gratitude for the gifts afforded them. The rituals that developed around this gratitude made perfect sense. I, too, was grateful for these gifts. That was how I knew that the native people and I shared the same passion.

I dug their arrowheads from the sandy creek flats and followed their bearing trees (or trail trees)—centuries-old oaks and hickories that a friend's grandfather told me the Indians had bent and tied down as saplings to mark the trail toward secret springs or caches of buried treasure for years to come. It seemed only natural that this land might teach me and mold me in a like way.

Whenever winter came, I waited for ice and snow to come to my forest. The magical day always stalked in under cover of night to ambush me the following morning with a frozen wellspring of joy. The world was transformed. The snow smoothed every sylvan scene as if by a gentle, omnipotent hand. The pines above were rimed in pale green crystal, bending down to my level as if beseeching me to come be a part of the masterpiece, arching to the perfect white mantle of the earth as though in prayer.

One of those days was my birthday—when I was twelve- or thirteen-winters-old. My running feet left the first human tracks in the pristine white of my front yard like the contrail of a spacecraft launching into the mysteries of outer space. When I reached my favorite part of the forest, I moved quietly through the altered spaces where tree trunks had converged overhead like low-ceiled cathedrals, and I felt some personal responsibility for the changed landscape, as though God had approved of my needful eye and arranged this natural wonder just for me.

This was my first preparation for tipi-life, for I saw the forest architecture as my true home: beams of wood leaning above me, intersecting at a solid confluence of buttresses. Chandeliers of refracted light sparkled overhead, even brighter than the snow. Even with my feet wet and cold, I stayed out late that evening, pushing the limits of my freedom, needing deep in my soul to see how this exquisite scene would change with the advent of night.

The darkness came and with it the moon. Annealing and bone-white, the growing orb rose and lit up everything around me like a warehouse of crystal sculptures. The forest took the lunar light as its own and turned it back on the world. The trees shimmered. The snow glowed from within, burning with a cold invisible flame.

Simple observations like this had stoked the fire in my soul, and I wanted such moments to last forever. As darkness spread across the sky, my mother's expectation that I show up for supper called me home. Still I lingered.

That was when the idea first hatched in my head— looking at these bending pines gilt in moonlight—that I would one day live simply beneath leaning trees. I never spoke about this. I didn't yet know the language that could explain such a notion. I tucked away the prophecy, went home, and eyed the squared-off walls, door frames, and carpets of our home. Now I knew that such angular things were not necessarily the natural way of all people. There are choices.

Coming home from that sacred day among winter pines, I probably smelled of pine resin and wet wool. I'm sure I carried snow crusted on my socks and the flush of winter on my cheeks. In our kitchen, Mama turned from the stove and smiled at me. It was the kind of smile you give a dirty-nosed puppy that's been digging relentlessly for a chipmunk.

Part of her probably wanted to know about my day, just a glimpse of it, so that she could assess my safety, I suppose. But another part gave me room. Drawn by the rich aroma, I went over to watch her stir a stew.

"You were born in the wrong time, weren't you, Mark." It was a statement more than a question.

"Yes, ma'am," I said, eager that she recognize who I was becoming.

"Well . . . I'm glad you weren't. I wouldn't have known you."

That simple exchange of words passed between us many times. It was a succinct one-act play of three lines that confirmed what lay at my center . . . and her approval of it. What would she have said if somehow I had been able to see into my future?

Mama, I'm going to live in a lot of unconventional places in my life—often bartering for rent. I'll need to do it because of the forests around them. That and to save money to buy the land where I will teach people about nature. For a couple of those years, I'm going to live in a tipi. I hope you'll be okay with that.

She dipped her spoon into the pot, and I watched her sample it. Her eyebrows arched to let me know it was good. As it turned out, she was okay with just about everything I did—including living in a tipi.

~ 3 ~

Home Equity

A few years before the old farmhouse burned, I had met a man from North Carolina who made tipis. He seemed a good place to start. When he and I first crossed paths, he had been inside one of his tipis, teaching a class on fire-making at a powwow. Always ready to learn better teaching techniques, I joined his group to see how he handled the lesson.

He was, in a word, a perfectionist—and happy for everyone to know it. His attention to detail and precision might have been admirable had he not been so officious about it. One visitor asked a question that the teacher must have considered unworthy of his time because he stared at his guest but didn't deign to answer. I felt embarrassed for both of them. The young man who had asked the question asked nothing more, and my attention drifted away from the lesson. Mostly I remember looking around at the tipi, soaking up the details.

I had reservations about calling, but the tipi was, after all, going to be my home. A precision product from a relentless perfectionist was probably a good idea. So I got to a telephone, dialed information, and made the call.

I first learned that there are several points to consider in customizing a tipi: size, type of canvas, weight of material, and fabric treatment options for mildew resistance or fire retardation. You must know your decision on all of these options before ordering. Of course, he didn't share these points with me so much as lecture me about them.

I began to remember the abrasive quality of his voice that had made me slip out early and attend another activity at the powwow. Beneath everything he said crept the underlying tone posing the same question: *What makes you think you have earned the right to live in one of my tipis?*

Before I could even explain what I needed, he cut me off. "You don't want to buy one of my tipis."

It was the last thing I expected to hear from him.

"I don't?"

"No."

"Why's that?"

"Too expensive for you."

Did something in my voice imply that I was destitute? I hadn't even mentioned the house fire.

"And how do you—"

"Just take my word for it. You don't want one of my tipis."

His silence took on the cold indifference of a cinderblock wall.

"Do you sell tipis very often?"

"Not very," he said stiffly.

Now, had he added, ". . . and I can't figure it out, you know? I make a damned good tipi . . . ," then I might have shared some marketing wisdom with him. But he didn't, so I thanked him for his time and hung up.

The next day, I mail-ordered a tipi from Colorado: just a simple phone call and a check in an envelope. No one even tried to talk me out of it.

~ 4 ~

Home Delivery

I once helped a friend make a tipi cover, cutting the roll of canvas into patterns and then sewing them together in a marathon of stitches. Laid out flat on the ground, it looked something like the lateral silhouette of a squat, thick-capped mushroom. The memory of the experience—and the attendant blisters—convinced me now that it was perfectly conscionable for me to purchase a cover this time. No one could say I hadn't paid the dues of the seamster. Besides, there would be plenty of work with the poles.

In those last decades of the twentieth century, a tipi cost a few hundred dollars. Purchasing ready-made poles from the manufacturer more than doubled that cost. I've never met a tipi dweller who bought the whole shebang. Which may have something to do with gender because the only tipi purchasers I've known have been male. In our culture, for better or for worse, sewing strongly ties to feminine traditions. Cutting, trimming, and sanding are another story. But both will blister the uninitiated, and both require dedication and finesse.

For men, reserving the tree work as personal labor may have more to do with feeling a rightful ownership of the home rather than the extra expense. Perhaps the same is true of women who buy their poles and sew the covers themselves. There is probably an inherent need among tipi-dwellers to look upon their abodes with some memory of sweat and labor to feel that the lodges truly belong to them.

I knew even before the tipi manufacturer pitched the poles as part of the package what I would say—even if he threw in a generous discount, which he did.

Two weeks later the cover arrived. It made for a ludicrous picture: a big cardboard box delivered to the concrete porch steps standing before the great pile of ash that had once been my house. You can imagine the UPS driver who left it there, looking around for a signature with nothing in sight to suggest that anyone lived there. On the other hand, if she read the label for the contents of the box, she probably would have put two and two together, grinning as she drove away.

The box was heavier than expected, its weight full of promise, as though I had really gotten my money's worth. Substantial as the box was, though, it didn't feel like the first in a string of new possessions. Tipis are living, working ephemera, often lasting only several years, putting aside the treatments and claims made by the manufacturer. Canvas has its enemies: UV rays in the meadow, mildew in the forest, fire anywhere in a lapse of attentiveness.

I cut open the box top to have a look, and the pungent smell of new canvas unfolded over me like a breath of relief at journey's end. The fabric was creamy white and folded neatly in thick slabs. As I lifted it from the box, the immaculate material radiated a virgin innocence that suggested we were starting out new together. I liked this feeling, a good alliance from the beginning. This pristine cloth looked to have no more experience with tipi-life than did I. It would never look this white again. In a sense, the same could have been said for me.

Everywhere I went those two years—a wedding, the hardware store, the courthouse to pay my taxes—I overheard someone mutter, "Is that smoke?" followed by squinting of eyes and looking around with some degree of alarm. "It is. I smell smoke!"

I grew so accustomed to the cling of woodsmoke to my skin, hair, and clothing that I accepted it as my permanent scent, reminded of it only when I left the woods for the civilized world. Of course, smoke was the perfect symbol for me for those two years. Smoke had directed me to a tipi. Now it was curing me of my eviction.

Through the eyes of native history, my transformation to tipi-dweller was much too easy: a huge prefolded mass of canvas left at my doorstep. A tipi-in-a-box. In the old days, these abodes consisted of hard-earned buffalo hides. I had invested no time in the training of my pony to match a violent buffalo stampede stride for stride, no shooting with my bow astride that pony at full gallop, no skinning, no hide scraping, no sewing with bone awl and sinew. Considering all the corners I had cut in acquiring the canvas, I wondered could it ever feel as though it was truly mine?

Still, there were the poles.

The Conversation

I do not do this lightly. I am filled with gratitude for your swift reach to the sun, slender and true, as great arrow shafts. Strong. I will labor over you with respect. Then I will honor you with my eyes each time I see you giving shape to my new home. You, the bones that stretch the skin of my shelter. Thank you for your strength and straightness."

I was whispering inside a stand of young Virginia pines rising vertically in a thicket of competing trunks. A bear would have had trouble squeezing through them. As I spoke to the trees, I cupped my hands to one of the trunks I planned to fell, skin to skin.

Tipi poles must be straight and taper slowly. Think of the tipi cover as an inverted conical paper cup with its point cut off. The cup has two holes: a large one that sits on the earth and a smaller top hole. Where the poles converge in a tipi, their individual diameters should be two inches or less so that their collective width does not exceed the size of the cover's top hole. If I had chosen just any tree, a twenty-foot pole cut with this snug convergence in mind might have a base over six inches thick. Such a pole would be too cumbersome to handle. *Pinus virginiana,* on the other hand, is sleek. Its proclivity to grow fast and therefore taper slowly produces a pole only an inch thicker at the base than at the apex. It is ideal.

After I had spoken my prayer of thanks, I took a gift from my pocket—called a "medicine bundle" by native people—and offered it by tying the little bag to one of the nearby pines that would remain. My gift consisted of items that have significance to me: fox fur, a sprig of hemlock, and a feather . . . all wrapped in tanned deer hide. To an observer, that solitary gesture might appear a little odd or, at best, wildly idiosyncratic. But I was simply speaking to the trees. The gift would remain long after my visit as a reminder of my interaction with this grove of trees.

In the 1970s, the forestry magazines published experiments that suggest trees communicate with one another, which came as more of a surprise to the public than it ought to have. Trees manufacture pheromones, variable chemical scents that carry messages on the wind. In fact, all plants—shrubs, herbs, ferns, vines, and even potted house plants—exchange silent messages. Animals, too, though this strikes most of us as less fantastic: the formic acid trail left by an ant, the pervasive spray of a skunk. It's not so terribly different from the habits of your family dog as it sprinkles tree after tree during your tandem evening walk. The musk in canine urine says: *My territory. Move on!*

The Cherokee, if only on instinct, understood this plant-talk phenomenon long before we non-natives considered it. Indeed, they took part in the sylvan dialogue, speaking to trees aloud. When they spoke of the trees, they called them "the Standing People."

The newly arrived Europeans must have thought the Cherokee deeply naive or childishly misguided in a pantheistic way. We must rethink that narrow-minded judgment. Early native people, it turns out, knew what they were doing. Their instincts in the natural world were usually much more potent and sustaining than the dwindling reservoir of similar knowledge in later, more refined cultures, such as ours. But go back far enough, and we all have ancestors who could boast such intimacy with nature. Those of us of European stock may still pick up messages without realizing it on a conscious level. We're being talked to, in other words; we just haven't been listening.

Is this so hard to believe? Women's menstrual cycles synchronize when they spend enough time together on a daily basis. Nor is this just the unusual occurrence of four women stranded in a snowbound cabin; it happens often enough in an office setting. Pheromones are at work all around us.

People who work with horses instruct their riders not to communicate fear to their mounts because experience shows that horses can sense it. They smell it. Conversely, in a tense situation, the calm of a rider can settle a horse without a word.

Whenever I discuss this phenomenon with adults at my wilderness school, it never fails to beg a question:

"But can pheromones cross the barrier between plants and animals?"

My response is always: "What barrier?"

Experiments have shown that people who regularly speak to their house plants see richer growth and healthier specimens. Perhaps some growers are encouraged to voice their love for their favorite plants because of the pleasant smell of its nectar, which is itself a pheromone designed specifically for such attraction . . . of insects. Potted plants also fare better when steeped in an ambience of classical music. Conversely, they suffer under the assault of heavy metal, refusing to flourish.

But is there a din of silent conversation in the forest all the time? Maples and sourwoods yakking away, Virginia pines chewing the fat? I doubt it. Wise in their ways, trees probably talk only when there is something important to talk about, much as smoke rises only when there is fire.

In the forestry commission experiment that revealed this sylvan code talk, one tree under duress warned other trees about a pending threat. A single tree was enclosed by a mesh net, into which was introduced a horde of leaf-ravaging insects. Delicate weighing devices that measured the density of leaf content had been attached to the leaves of surrounding trees. When the sacrificial tree began to be devoured, the leaves of nearby trees became lighter in weight.

But what did this mean?

Bystander trees had clearly responded to an alert sent out by the ravaged tree. The bystanders then withdrew the sugary juices from their own leaves by pulling that sweetness into their harder-to-access woody parts. What remained in the leaves were the natural chemicals meant to ward off predators. Expecting unwanted leaf-eaters, the trees mustered a proactive response, making their leaves not only less palatable but outright defensive. The medium of the message was pheromones.

In other experiments, plants have even been shown to detect a person's mood, suggesting that a human's presence in the forest does not go unnoticed by the surrounding flora. Our passage through nature is not announced merely by a barking squirrel, a bolting rabbit, or an airborne rippling of sparrows. There's a more poignant discourse going on. The trees are alive and quietly aware . . . of us.

Reading these studies, it stunned me to realize that for the lifetime I had spent in the forest, I had never really been alone. Much of that woods-time I had spent in stalking mode, just to see what I could see. By shifting to the painstaking slowness of a stalker, I had minimized my impact upon the forest, my foot pressing against the earth not as a mindless tread but as a mindful choice—a gentle touch, you might say. Wherever my feet sensed an obstacle to passage, I adjusted the route of my snail's pace to spare the forest even the slightest sound, which usually equates to damage. As a stalker I floated through the landscape without leaving a careless trail.

Had this attitude opened a secret door to the wild, allowing new depths of intimacy or belonging? It had always felt that way. And are there human pheromones that are manufactured to accompany this increased respect for the plants and animals? Experiments suggest this to be so.

My students often confess that being in the woods calms them. Such an experience lies at the other end of the spectrum of a business-as-usual day with traffic, cell phones, deadlines, TV, appointments, and a constant stream of noise. They always speak of this pacifying experience as a one-way equation, the human benefiting from the wild. Yet could there be a flow of information running in the other direction, too?

Each of us is a contained body swimming with myriad chemicals and boiling with their reactions to one another. Each physiological process that goes on inside us requires its specific formula of chemical interaction, whether it's digestion, fight or flight, deep emotion, blood production, etc. We're a walking warehouse of chemistry. Whatever ingredients bubble up for the recipe at hand—say, extreme jealousy—involve a telltale scent, even if we don't consciously register it. These days, plants may know more about our natural biological smells than we do.

Living in a tipi delivered me to a higher plateau of mindfulness about plants. Suspended periods of respect, you could call it. My movements inside the lodge were naturally quiet and respectful to the space in which I lived.

This was my habit when touching foot to earth. When I stepped outside, that same grace of motion went with me, dictating every move.

Committing to tipi-life is a kind of defection in which you wander into another culture. You shake off the last remnants of life on autopilot and embrace the aliveness that has been waiting here in the wild for anyone who takes time to recognize it. My own awakening, I believe, began inside this grove of Virginia pines because I was taking these trees with me into my new life. The sacrifice demanded my respect

The ceremony complete, I picked up my hatchet and, for two hours, felled seventeen trees. Then I dragged away the first pair toward the chosen site where my tipi would stand.

Would the result have been any different had I simply leapt into the task without pause or ceremony, taking ax to the trees? Seventeen trees would have fallen just the same. Does the way we do things change the result?

For me, certainly, yes. I cannot speak for the trees, cannot prove that there is a logic to this method. All I can say is that, having gone to the heart of the forest, anything short of mindfulness and reverence for my own interactions would have been unacceptable. The gift-giving ritual, when I learned about it, reached out to me with the same common sense as saying "thank you" to a person who has done me a favor.

~ 6 ~

Bones of Wood

Pole preparation is formidable, requiring a week and a half of continuous work just for the *first* phase: debarking and smoothing the pine trunks. I worked all day, every day. Some people spread out the task over a year, but their tipis were going to be second homes that would enjoy only occasional use. Mine was my dwelling, a womb inside the cold weather, a roof from every rain. Having your house burn down just before autumn might be the surest way to inspire a rock-solid work ethic, in case you don't already have one.

Two by two, I leaned into the work of dragging the crudely trimmed pines a quarter mile through the tall late summer grasses to the back of the meadow. Growing there were two waist-thick pines to which I lashed a crossbeam to serve as a support bench for each pole as I worked on it.

Each time I returned for two more poles, my dragging trail through the grass took on the semblance of a growing tribe passing my way—a migration. Elly walked beside me, oblivious to the history of her species' part in this process. Dogs once dragged shorter, lighter poles for the nomads of the Plains, though not in these Georgia mountains, where the tipi hadn't made an appearance until latter-day enthusiasts like me used them.

Seventeen trees, and hundreds of branches to trim— each cut from below, toward the top of the tree, to prevent gouges ripped from the trunk. It was a sizable task, but this wasn't my first time preparing poles. I had done it several times before in the erection of community tipis for camps, so I knew the amount of work in store. Even with several helpers in those camps, it had been taxing. This time I was alone. Exactly as it should be. It was to be my home and no one else's—or so I thought.

Seventeen poles, one at a time. When I had finished one, if I had done it right, that one pole would stand as a chore of the past. Complete. Not to be revisited. Done.

Sixteen poles. Do this one right, too. Do it only once. Then fifteen poles, and fourteen. It was likely going to be my abode for a long time. These were my supports. The work was an investment. Get it right the first time. No correcting a job poorly done. Thirteen poles, then twelve. And so it went.

After de-limbing and lashing a pole to the crossbeam came debarking. The local hardware store stocked the ideal tool—a drawknife—at forty-nine dollars new. But at a mountain flea market, I found an old-fashioned one: a finer-made version that could be sharpened by hand rather than by machine. It cost eight dollars.

A good drawknife glides and slices with a certain elegance. Even with its double-handled, lopsided design, it has a pleasing balance. The bark surrenders gracefully, sailing down to the ground in strips. It demands some muscle, but the fluidity of motion becomes almost hypnotic.

It is satisfying work but almost impossible to perform without acquiring a second skin of sticky pine sap. The direction of the knife in use encourages sap to spit all over the bark-scraper. With the luxury of old clothes, I could have sacrificed a set to a resinous fate. But heavenly fire denied me that luxury, so I worked shirtless with an old rag stuffed in the waistband of my jeans like a loincloth. By the end of that week and a half of nonstop labor, sap had dried on my skin to a dark, abiding crust, making me feel as tough as a woods bison inside and out. My jeans were stiff enough to stand up on their own at night as I dreamed of endless strokes and stubborn, woody knots.

The poles lay in a stack off the ground on a makeshift rack. They dried for three weeks, my reward for the ten days of intensive, exhaustive blade work. During this time, down at the river, I scrubbed at the patches of body hair cemented to my skin by the sap. I spent half my days in the Etowah, lathering up with sweet pepperbush leaves, trying to crack the tough hide that I had acquired. For more abrasive action, I even added sand to the mix. But the more I scrubbed, the less the toughness of buffalo hummed inside me. Those days, I felt more like a freshly skinned opossum tossed into a boiling cook pot.

After sanding myself, it was time to sand the poles. Each one had to be flawlessly smooth—and not just to prevent abrading or puncturing the tipi cover. If you have never slept in a tipi during a rainstorm, you cannot fully appreciate the need for excellence in this stage of the pole-work. It's the smoothness of the poles that keeps the interior of the tipi dry. Hastily worked poles, on the other hand, will guarantee ceaseless dripping of water into the lodge.

The apex of a tipi cover wraps tightly around the convergence of the poles, but raindrops striking the exposed tops of the poles will run through that juncture down into the tipi. If the poles are meticulously smooth, each water droplet will adhere to the underside of the slanted wood and ride the pole all the way to the ground at the periphery of the living space. But if the droplet encounters a single nick, bump, or splinter, it will break loose and free-fall from the blemish in question. Further, there is an unwritten law about tipi pole flaws: If there is only one drip, it will materialize directly above your bed at midnight during a storm.

If you find yourself in that rude predicament, that dripping, errant streamlet from the pole can be encouraged to stay on the wood by wetting a path for it down the underside of the pole with a finger. Touch the next bead of water that forms, and, before it drips off, smear it down the pole finger-paint-style. Water has an affinity for cohesion as well as adhesion. It's almost miraculous to see it happen. Give the drip-spot a watery track, and it's a good bet that the next droplet and those after will follow the wet path on the pole rather than disengage from it. Though I did not know it at the time, for the next few months after moving in, many a night I would be finger-painting my way back to a drip-less sleep, then later resanding problem poles until finally all were perfect.

Virginia pines are more rot resistant than some trees but only at their core, so a preservative must boost the longevity of tipi poles. Tung oil, from the tropical tung tree, was my choice. I applied it with my old loincloth rag. By the time I finished this phase of the work, I knew that if I fell over dead and was not found for decades in the back of the meadow, my hands would remain well-preserved. In fact, they might never decompose. I was convinced that centuries later I could be identified by my fingerprints.

In the old days on the Great Plains, it was the women who did all this tipi work. The men killed the buffalo.

Later, once Europeans had reintroduced horses to the continent (a much smaller, terrier-sized horse had long ago gone extinct in North America), the men hauled freshly cut lodge pole pines from the mountains by horseback, dropped the rough stack at the feet of their wives, and then most likely embarked on a well-timed, epic antelope hunt that might last a moon or more, leaving the women to do all the hide-work and the scraping and smoothing of those all-important poles.

Throughout this project, those women lingered in my mind. They had no drawknife, after all, no sandpaper, no bucket of tung oil, no easy-to-come-by rags. (My few strips of cloth came from my friend Teresa, whose laundry room became my vault of priceless scrap dish towels.) These women had no big box of pristine canvas delivered to their doors. Instead they hiked out to the corpse-strewn scene of a buffalo hunt, skinned the enormous creatures, stretched and staked out the skins under the prairie sky, and scraped both sides with tools of sharpened bone or stone to remove hair, epidermis, muscle, fat, blood, membrane, and endodermis until only the dermis was left.

After the scraping, the skin dried to rawhide, as hard and tough as a modern ABS plastic canoe. With a lot of vigorous rubbing, they saturated the rawhide with oils from the buffalo's brain. Now wet and flaccid again, the hide was stretched more tightly inside a frame of pegs pounded into the earth. The skin was further stretched by kneading it with the rounded end of a thick stick—the women leaning their weight into it as it slowly dried again. Stubborn spots too stiff for brain oil were often chewed into submission. Again, women's work.

In the next phase of this work, the brain-wet, sloppy skin—constantly stretched—passed through a remarkable transformation. As it stretched and dried, the hide eventually became a soft, chamois-like material with a fluffy nap pleasing to the touch.

Finally the skins had to be smoked over a smudge fire. Otherwise, when wetted, a skin would revert to tough, hard rawhide, and all that braining and stretching would have to be repeated. Inundating every skin fiber with smoke-borne resin prevented this disaster. This step waterproofed each skin fiber, but it didn't waterproof the skin as a whole. To that end, the women crushed buffalo hooves in hot water, let it sit, and then skimmed off the neat's-foot oil that rose to the top. They rubbed this oil into the skin until it could repel water.

I have prepared plenty of deerskins this way. One deerskin is a lot of work. A single buffalo skin, I imagine, requires ten times the effort. To say nothing of the dozen buffalo skins needed for a single tipi.

When the wood had absorbed the tung oil, I set about to erect the poles. First I laid the cover on the ground, interior-side up, and laid three poles carefully on top, lashed together to form an asymmetrical X—one stroke of the X consisting of two poles paired together. A clove hitch bound the three poles at their common juncture, and I left the long trailing rope uncut. By driving pegs into the ground before the bases of these poles and pulling on the rope, I hoisted the contraption upright and then swung one of its double-legs outward to make a tripod, the clove hitch tightening as the legs spread.

It was a landmark moment: my new home defined into its rudimentary pyramidal space, suggesting the size it would take on as I ringed the others poles into a cone. As always with a tipi, it was taller, grander, and statelier than I had anticipated.

Native Americans had a formulaic pattern—an order—for adding on those remaining poles, which is no random stacking. It was a method worked out by the Plains women centuries ago, and anyone who erects a tipi today, if he or she is smart, still follows this pattern. In fact, my tipi cover arrived with these same historic instructions, showing the sequence for stacking the poles to allow for the least collective bulk of the poles at their point of convergence.

By tradition the Plains people oriented their tipis to the rising sun, the door facing east. One tripod pole stood just to the left of the door, another at due north, and the third at south. The first loose pole was positioned at the right of the door and then three more were spaced in sequence toward the north tripod pole. These first four poles leaned into the front crotch made by the convergence of the tripod. The next four marched from the left door pole back to the south, their tops fitting into an adjacent crotch above. Three more poles filled out the back, running from north to south, leaving a gap in the center for the lifting pole, which would hoist the cover skyward. These last poles leaned into the rear crotch, completing the clever consolidation of poles at the apex of the cone.

I followed the formula and watched the tripod fill out and tighten into the backward leaning, asymmetrical cone inherent of tipi design. When all but the lifting pole were up, I walked the loose end of the rope around and around the outside of the cone, flipping it at intervals to snap it taut to the juncture of the poles by a contiguous series of tight coils. When I had made four orbits, I walked the trailing end of the rope inside the cone, tied the rope to a two-foot-long wooden peg carved from yellow locust, and hammered the peg into the ground at an angle until the rope was snug, anchoring the framework securely to the earth.

Years before, I had visited a tipi set up in a grassy area by a friend. He wasn't at home, so as I waited I gathered some firewood for him and stacked it inside his lodge. I noticed that his anchor rope dangled downward into a loose coil by his fire pit. It wasn't staked.

Soon dark clouds gathered overhead and gusts of wind began laying the tall grass on its side and molding my flapping shirt and pants against my body like a second skin. This wind roared with a ferocity that served as the perfect soundtrack for what happened next. The tipi launched straight into the air like a clunky, primitive rocket. Disconnected from the earth, hovering and silhouetted against that dark, dramatic sky, it was a phantasm—a whimsical illustration from some children's bedtime story. The tipi lifted vertically thirty feet into the air, poles and all, before turning back on itself in a smooth arc and nose-diving back to earth with a crash barely heard over the wind from thirty yards away.

All my friend's belongings were suddenly exposed to the world. It was a comic picture, seeing his bed and stacks of clothes stranded all alone on a grassy meadow. I thought of the classic photo of Marilyn Monroe standing over a sidewalk steam vent with a rascally mind of its own. But I didn't laugh at the work ahead. The rain arrived without mercy and began drenching everything.

Upwardly mobile home. Memorable. It was a lesson I took to heart.

Hearthstone

With the framework of my lodge established, I tied the top of the tipi cover to one of the three unused poles, the sturdiest one, which I had set aside for hoisting the heavy canvas. Then, after folding the cover into long pleats, I levered pole and cover upward, settling the pole into its appointed notch at the rear of the tipi and, finally, unfurling the canvas around the frame like two great wings spreading and enfolding a nest of eggs. The seams met in front with their overlapping double rows of lacing holes gratifyingly aligned. Into the holes went horizontal wooden stays I'd carved from dogwood. With the stays in place, this fastening of the front seam—above and below the open oval doorway—was, in essence, a kind of primitive stitching . . . but with wood.

At the base of the tipi cover, I pushed a pebble into the canvas and gathered the material around it, covering the stone, tied it off with cord, and staked the cord to the earth. This was probably the earliest method of securing the cover to the ground. I did the same in nine more places. By the time I had made a complete circuit, the canvas circumference was so tight at ground level that it put undue tension on the poles, causing the material to ride up them, much the way a low-slung holster belt tries to climb from a person's hips to his waist. Seeing the problem, I wrestled the cover groundward and reset the loosened stakes at a sharper angle. I'm betting that the native woman who first designed sewn-on loops at the bottom of a tipi cover made quite a name for herself.

With the cover finally snug over the poles and held fast just inches above the ground, I fitted the last two poles into the pockets of the smoke flaps. These are rectangular flaps that project forward from the gap in the cover where smoke escapes. Their long poles angle from outside the back of the lodge and around the side to nose into pockets sewn into the upper corners of the flaps. They are almost like tilted flagpoles—but rather than the pole supporting the flag, the flag supports the pole. By weight and tension these poles stretch the flaps taut. The variable placements of these two poles control the flow of smoke from the tipi by louvering the flaps to accommodate the direction of the wind. Or, if no fire is wanted, the flaps can be crossed over one another to virtually plug the smoke hole.

But I wasn't done yet. There was still a door to mount . . . as well as the inside liner, which rises almost halfway up the tipi's height from the ground. I decided to put that off until later. I needed a break.

It is said that a squaw could erect her family's tipi in less than a half hour. I was well into my second hour, but that was okay. I was enjoying the process, savoring every detail and soaking up the reasoning for each aspect of the task. Best of all, I didn't have a husband to scowl at my slow progress.

Inside I viewed the convergence of my efforts, and a homeowner's satisfaction began to glow within me. The bracing of the poles looked strong and stable. The shape of the living space beckoned. I looked up at a triangle of blue sky through the opening of the smoke flaps and could hardly wait to experience my first inside-fire that night. I would need to dig a fire pit, of course, and ring it with stones. Directly opposite my sleeping place, I wanted a large, flat upright rock to throw the heat back toward me, like a mirror in a dark room reflecting light back into it.

I'd had my eye on a big slab of stone half-buried in the steep north slope running down to the river. From the moment I'd spotted it, I knew it would be my reflector stone. I backed away from the tipi and visualized the night settling in around the luminescence of the fire. *How much firelight would show through the canvas?* I wondered. *Would the tipi light up like a lantern?* I imagined smoke streaming through the flaps, trailing out over the valley from the ridge top. I turned and walked with purpose toward that rock.

Budging the rock—ever so slightly—from its resting place, I could see this was going to be a herculean task: a quarter mile up a very steep hill with a heavy hunk of stone that felt dense as a slab of iron. But it was the perfect shape, and I knew that no other rock would do. Just over three inches thick, two-and-a-half feet by two feet and shaped with a gentle curve, it was beautiful. Once I had dug this stone out of the earth, there was no going back.

As it was, I had already invested half an hour of my "break" into its excavation.

I elevated the rock by stages. Kneeling on one leg, I propped the behemoth stone on one edge, slid it by quarter inches up the angle of my knelt thigh, heaved it to the higher thigh, wedged it into my lap, and stood while keeping my back vertical. Then, with a guttural grunt and biceps pulling out all the stops, I hugged the monster to my chest and began the trek up the mountain to my camp.

At best the journey uphill was a sustained stagger. Stopping to rest was out of the question. I didn't want to test my spine against that lift again. So on I trudged.

Despite all this—weight, climb, potential orthopedic hazards—there was a profound simplicity to the act. I was lugging a spine-crunching rock up a mountain not unlike Sisyphus—except that my efforts, I hoped, would bring a satisfying conclusion. The equation was direct: I needed heat this winter; this rock would reflect it from my fire; I needed this rock on the ridge, so I carried it there. A primal syllogism.

Under more ordinary circumstances, I might have achieved domestic heat by turning five or six corners: Drive to a school to present a nature program; take the students outside to reinforce the lessons from the classroom; pick up a check from the school secretary on my way out; stop at the bank on the way home to deposit the check. Twice a year I would write a personal check to the local gas company that came out in a big truck to refill the huge propane tank that fueled the fifty-year-old space heaters in the old farmhouse. Turn a valve, scratch a match, and *whump*! Heat.

But now I was straining with the honest weight of stone, my hands clutched like talons against the grit, hugging this bone-crunching prize to my chest, plodding purposefully up a mountain, each step like my working of the poles—something I would never have to repeat, one step at a time, accountable. The reward pressed against me, palpable, rock to chest, rock to tipi. No middleman—just me, earning the heat of winter with muscle and sweat.

Simplicity and accountability aside, there was something slightly preposterous about my mission. As I inched my way ever upward, I kept thinking about the sage old saying often laughed about around the campfires of these mountains: "Indian keeps warm with small fire. White man keeps warm running around for lots of wood for big fire." Had I taken the truth of that aphorism to a whole new level?

Every muscle in my body was screaming when I topped out above the slope and stepped upon the blessed horizontal relief of the meadow. The tipi was still sixty yards away. On that last leg of the haul, I was like a decrepit soul staggering from the lowest rung of the Inferno carrying an overambitious souvenir. The walk across the meadow seemed interminable. My biceps were knots, my legs turning rubbery, my lower spine threatening like a brittle stick.

Entering the low oval doorway, I bent at the knees to salvage my back. My legs nearly collapsed. Very carefully, I lowered one knee to the ground and eased the stone into its appointed place at the fire pit, the concave surface aimed at my bed site like a benevolent hand cupped to gather heat, throwing it my way for all the nights to come. Relief poured through my body. I was feather-light. I imagined my aching vertebrae expanding like an accordion sucking in air. Packing smaller stones into the dirt, I shored up the great stone until it was stable. Then I crawled around to my sleeping place, lay on my side, and gazed at my prized slab of stone for thirty solid minutes.

That propane tank from my former life sat alone like a comical, pint-sized, silver submarine dry-docked beside the pile of ash and debris that once had been my house. Shiny and metallic, it looked ridiculous next to the rubble: a memorial to the folly of best-laid plans. Throughout the next year, whenever I passed through the old gate to the county road, I glanced over at the bulbous tank and remembered my odyssey with the reflecting rock, a compact monolith at the center of my home, throwing heat to my bed even when the fire that it had absorbed had gone out.

It would be the following summer when I was painting a pictograph on the tipi canvas that a truck arrived at the front of the property. I was completely absorbed in my work, basking in the success of my primitive artistic tools. The brush was a carved stick with a tuft of deer hairs attached by pine-pitch glue, while three box turtle shells contained the plant dyes I had mixed. Across the wooded valley came the grind of machinery and voices yelling over it. Pulled out of my reverie, I set down my paints and listened. A motor whined; it sounded like an electric hoist. I heard the clank of metal on metal. By the time I had walked out there to see what was happening, the workmen were gone. And so was the propane tank.

I stood looking at the empty space where the tank had recently stood, and I thought once again of my journey up the mountain with the hearthstone hugged to my chest. I couldn't hear an engine anywhere off in the distance, the truck long since gone.

"That was easy," I said and walked back to finish my painting.

~ 8 ~

First Night

Throughout all my work with the poles, Elly had lounged in the grass, seemingly content to hear the scrape of my drawknife. Between naps she traipsed away on half-hearted excursions in search of voles or chipmunks. She was no help, but I can't fault her. She almost never preferred sleeping in the tipi. If it rained, she came inside. If it thundered, she trembled uncontrollably and walked all over me with wet and nervous paws. Sparing a storm, she always preferred sleeping outside. Perhaps she took pride in taking her night watch.

Without any maudlin exhibitions of dependence or forfeiture of her canine instincts to survive, Elly transcended the man's-best-friend role. Her sweet brown eyes made instant friends of strangers and validated her devotion to me on a daily basis. Those same eyes, ever alert, could find me anywhere.

Her nose was a tracking phenomenon. There was no place I could hide from her for long. At thirty-six pounds, she was as fit as an Olympian, without being high-strung like so many other athletic dogs. If I could run like the wind, she was lightning. She pledged herself to me totally yet held to her animal mystique, remaining one of the most individualistic beings I have ever known. She chose to be *with* me, as her behavior affirmed again and again; but it was she who set the rules of that partnership, like sleeping alone outside the lodge.

There is a long-standing history between tipis and dogs. The first tipis of the Great Plains were quite small, requiring the inhabitants to stoop even after entering. The size of the abode was dictated by the strength of the only animal they had domesticated: *Canis familiaris,* the camp dog. Plains tribes were migratory, following the buffalo, and the tipi was the continent's first portable breakdown tent. In that nomadic lifestyle, you could keep only what you could carry, and, until the Spanish reintroduced the horse to the Americas, the dog was the beast of burden upon which tipi poles were lashed as a dragging sled for hauling gear. That sled bears a name contributed by the French-Canadian trappers: a travois, pronounced either trav-WAH or tré-VOY, the same root word also giving us "travail," or painfully difficult work.

To be historically correct about the original tipi, picture not heavy twenty-foot-long, horse-drawn poles but much thinner seven- to nine-foot-long saplings that could be lashed to a dog. Maybe Elly's genetic legacy was whispering to her from the past. Maybe she knew her place in the story. This huge cone I had erected wasn't *her* tipi. Until I brought a horse into the family, any hauling of these oversized parts was clearly my job.

Perhaps the choice of a tipi isn't so authentic for a white, Anglo-Saxon naturalist—especially here in the East, where tipis were never used by native people. But it was a gratefully borrowed design, and already I was in love with the idea of living in it. There is a secretive womblike privilege to sleeping in one—much like what I used to feel as a child when, on a rainy day, I'd set up the card table in our family den, drape a blanket over it, and time-travel to far-flung outposts in history.

When I knelt, stepped through the doorway of my new tipi, and then straightened to behold the tall leaning poles, an unexpected sense of liberation washed through my spine. I had grown accustomed to stooping in that little borrowed dome tent that had broken down. The freedom to stroll around the circle of my new home, fully upright, was like being released from a cramped cage back into the wild.

Quietly I moved around and around the fire pit, passing through the space as though it were a medium more rarefied than air. Each of the pie-piece segments of the floor where I was stepping in time would become allocated to some utilitarian purpose—with storage spaces along the periphery—but the immediate ring around the fire pit always remained open. That circle of earth was more intimate to me than any real estate claimed by contract or tender.

All that was missing in my annular stroll was a sun to center my orbit. So I sat down and began arranging sticks in the fire pit. First, four small forked branches impaled into the earth—standing only inches high. Then two pencil-size parallel rafters set into the upstanding Ys. Then five cross-rafters completed a raised shelf. All this wood was gathered from oak or some other hardwood—thick, dense pieces that would not readily burn.

Next came the kindling—the smallest branchlets of white pine and hemlock and tulip tree. A tacit ceremony enveloped the entire process. The quiet was sacrosanct to the occasion. The first fire in any tipi might be compared to cracking a champagne bottle against the prow of a virgin ship, but the thought that goes into it—the practiced piecing together of the pyre, the reverential silence, the glorious mystery of flames that move as if alive, licking and consuming—all these factors elevate this christening, it seems to me, to be a more powerful ritual yet.

Around this scaffold of kindling, I began a new design, concentric to the one in which I sat, one stick at a time, laid carefully, just like the tipi poles. Indeed, the finished pyre was a tipi itself—albeit a wooden one. Though complete and ready for a match, a match wouldn't do. The occasion whispered a demand for something more.

The first fire inside my tipi should be done the old way, I knew. This was more than a home. It was a graphic history book that had opened its pages and swallowed me whole.

Fire is a hypnotic medium. Ancient scientists categorized it neither as solid nor liquid nor gas, but rather as plasma. Where did it come from? How could it be drawn from a slab of dead wood? In the old days, natives phrased it something like this: "In the Long Ago, certain of the trees swallowed fire and stored it deep inside their wood. If you know how to ask in the proper way, that tree will give up its fire for you."

Charming, one might think; but, again, Native American philosophies contain subtleties that bear a second look, like calling trees "the Standing People." Many are quick to assume that the name derives from the statuesque nature of trees that stand above and dwarf us. But could it be that early Americans knew about photosynthesis by some primal instinct that explained how the world runs on solar energy? Might that name be describing the sublime talent that trees possess in making their own food rather than wandering around in search of it? Trees do not hunt or forage. They stand rooted and resolute in their perfect and enviable autonomy. Don't trees swallow the fire of the sun? When wood burns, is it not surrendering all those photons of energy that the tree's leaves once snatched from sunlight and eventually stored within woody fiber?

With my knife I smoothed a stiff stalk of dead mullein and test-spun it between my hands, palm facing palm. It spun true. This would be my fire-making drill. Then, into a slab of dead juniper, I cut a small dime-size slot to receive the end of the drill and hold it in one place.

After half a minute of spinning and grinding the drill into the juniper, smoke began to curl—just a wisp, the first trace of smoke in a lodge whose scent and colors would one day bear testament to the many resins released from burning oak, maple, hickory, sourwood, and dogwood.

It was time to cut the all-important notch into the juniper, where hot ash could pour into the nest of tinder I had kneaded into fluff from the inner bark of a dead basswood branch. I set the tinder in place and prepared for the warrior phase of the project—drilling with serious intent and persevering until the notch was filled with smoking ash.

When I blew my tinder into a flame and set it under the pyre in the pit, the crackle of wood spoke like an ancient, familiar voice, filling the space as though the tipi had been holding its breath, waiting for a fire to release it from silence, giving it life.

How many times had I made fire this way, demonstrating for my students? Too many to count. But this fire was like my first, releasing something inside me. I became acutely aware of my place in a chain that began with the sun. This fire had traveled through space from sun to Earth, soaked into a tree, then transferred through my hands into my fire pit, finally to imbue my home with its first natural colors. I was painting with strokes of the sun.

Smoke rose from the center of the fire pit as I thought about the word *hearth*. Embedded inside that word lay two others: *heart* and *earth,* each differing by just one letter placement, a kind of symmetry forming between the two inside the larger word.

Is fire the heart of the earth? It is certainly the center of community. Watch any group of people at night around a campfire, and the question will answer itself. And don't geologists tell us that fire smolders at the core of the Earth?

There should be a story, I thought to myself, about those select trees from which skilled hands can elicit fire, a story about roots probing deep, searching for relief from a drought, only to venture too far and tap into the fiery center of the planet. In such a way are myths born, I realized.

Twilight thickened to darkness outside as my newly inhabited tipi took on an independence of luminosity—a separate world able to provide proof against the night without presuming to conquer it. I stepped outside and waited to see the tipi glow as full darkness settled in. I was right; it was a little like a lantern, if less imposing. More like a candle inside a paper bag.

That first night forever changed me. I lay on my back and studied the altered look of the white canvas painted in sepia tones by the glow of my fire. The narrow triangle of night sky bordered by the smoke flaps was my window. The long-tapering poles—those Virginia pines that I had cut, trimmed, scraped, and smoothed over weeks— converged with a kind of tribal synergy. They huddled like a community putting its heads together to solve a problem.

It was like gazing up into a great distance measured by parallel lines and the illusion of their coming together at some faraway point. The poles towered, took on a semblance of being alive. Against the canvas, their shadows jumped and quivered at the whim of the unpredictable flames. The hypnotic movement almost formed a pattern but not quite.

Stars looked back at me through the triangle. Only a few, but never had I been so connected to stars. Woodsmoke rose clean as it rushed to meet the cool ether of summer's end. River shoals deep in the valley rose to my ears like a whispered explanation from each stone that parted the water. A screech owl warbled its lament from the edge of the meadow, its song descending like a twirling spiral of loose rope. These sounds heightened the silence inside my home. But it wasn't like listening to the night from a room through a window; I wasn't separate from these sounds, just as I wasn't removed from the night.

Why was that? I wondered.

The moon had been blossoming like a white flower on the canvas until it sailed into view against the blackness. It began a slow journey across the triangular opening of the smoke flaps, its celestial eye looking in on me, welcoming. My life sidestepped from the march of seconds and minutes—even centuries. I had become timeless. I could have been anywhere, anyone, at any time.

It was hard to sleep with all this newness, and that was just as well. I didn't want to miss any of it. I stayed with the moon just as it stayed with me, eyeball-white and unblinking until, the baptismal event complete, it passed beyond the triangle. It had marked my place on the ridge, accepted me. Now the triangle darkened again, releasing the stars to their slow turn across the heavens.

The coals in the pit glowed orange-red. I carefully selected which sticks to burn next and watched them smoke and then leap into yellow flame. The fire crackled in tiny pops and snaps. In the mountain-cool night, the heat from the flames, like a dry liquid, conformed to every curve and facet of my face. Against my closed eyes it rippled across my flesh, and I watched ghostly shapes flicker through the blood-field of my eyelids. Ancient dancers.

With perfect economy, heat radiated from the large, concave reflector-stone. Carrying it here had been like planting a seed from which this new home could sprout. This fire was the center of my life. It beat an ancient pulse that the earth had held deep in its gut. Heart, earth, hearth.

My stack of firewood towered high—the size of a winter bear sleeping in the shadows. I was rich, for there was nothing else that I needed or wanted. This was the first night, and I felt blessed to know that there would be more. As many more as I chose.

9

First Morning

In the dark I opened my eyes and waited, lying very still. The coals in the fire pit were covered by a mound of gray ash, but a pleasing breath of radiant warmth bathed the left side of my face. Birds rustled in the trees. The forest was waking. At first light, the poles defined themselves into a great tower soaring upward above me. It was unlike any architecture that I had ever beheld. They stood black against the grainy gray of the canvas, rising as though they were growing. Then they leaned together, wove at the confluence, and spread again like a hand opened in morning prayer to the sky.

The picture was full of grace and, though static, an illusion of upward movement. I lay there and stared, knowing already that this image had branded itself into my memory. I will never forget that morning. I will always remember what it was to be at the center of that circle.

Teresa visited later that morning to check on my progress. Dressed for work, she resembled a time-traveler who had slipped through a seam in history to revisit the past. She was surprised to see the project completed. I didn't mention that Lakota women would have had the structure up weeks ago.

"Well," she said, smiling at my obvious pride in my new home, "how is it?"

I studied my working tipi and shook my head in awe of the integration of its parts. There were no proper words for it.

"You should try it. It takes you to a place you've never been but you knew you wanted to visit."

Her smile turned to a mischievous lift of an eyebrow. "So where's the shower and hot water?" she said, out of place with her carefully brushed hair, immaculate wardrobe, and fancy shoes—the last of which she had enough to fill the firewood space in the tipi's floor plan.

"You might have to get up a little earlier than usual. You'd have to heat it by the saucepan-ful."

She gave me a look. "Right."

"Oh, the saucepan doesn't have a handle. You might want to allow another hour for that."

"Why doesn't it have a handle?"

"I found it that way . . . in a junk pile."

"I'll bring you one," she called out, waving, as she returned to her car. "I have an extra."

I turned to admire my tipi again, this time trying to see it through her eyes. I laughed quietly. *Teresa would never make a tipi woman,* I thought, *but her saucepan will fit in just fine.*

But then I broke out of my reverie. There was work to do. Last night a mouse had invaded my granola. I spent the morning building a rodent-proof cairn of stacked stones—a cereal sepulcher, if you will. Problem solved, but that wasn't the last of the critters I would have to deal with.

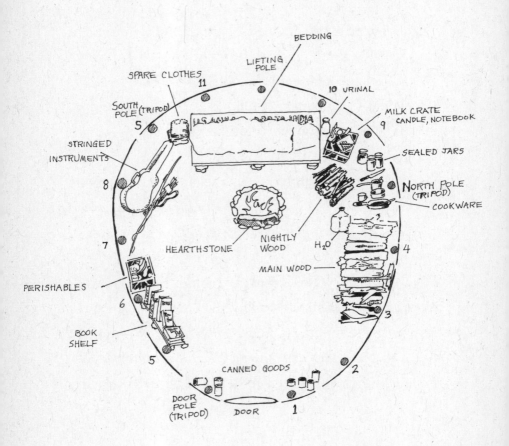

BEDDING

LIFTING
POLE

SPARE CLOTHES

11

SOUTH
POLE (TRIPOD)

S

10 URINAL

MILK CRATE
9 CANDLE, NOTEBOOK

STRINGED
INSTRUMENTS

8

SEALED JARS

NORTH POLE
(TRIPOD)

COOKWARE

7

HEARTHSTONE

NIGHTLY
WOOD

H₂O

MAIN WOOD

4

PERISHABLES

6

3

BOOK
SHELF

5

CANNED GOODS

2

DOOR
POLE
(TRIPOD)

DOOR

1

A Round Space

Autumn drifted into the mountain meadow. Friends at High Meadows Camp took messages for me so that I could keep working off-season. A school, scout troop, or garden club would call, request a program, and the message fell into a wooden box carved with my name—made for me by a camper at the arts and crafts workbench.

Twice a week I traveled to the nearest pay phone, eight miles away. There I pushed a pocketful of change into the coin slots, checked in with the camp, dug for more coins, returned calls to prospective clients, and finalized the jobs.

Before the house fire, I had been hosting three-day camping trips for elementary, high school, and college classes. I had developed crucial relationships with several Montessori schools that wanted to expand their curricula with regular outdoor programs. One in particular formed a symbiotic bond with me. More than twenty-five years later, Arbor Montessori remains my most dedicated client, and I their appreciative outdoor educator.

On the days that I didn't host classes, I worked on Native American crafts to replace items lost in the fire. These replicas were essential to my programs. I also ratcheted up the gears in looking for land to purchase. I wasn't going to be able to develop fully my own wilderness school on someone else's property.

Feeling perched on the edge of time, I moved back and forth between two worlds. In the schools I visited, I lived by the period-changing bell. Back at my tipi, the path of the sun and moon, the slow turn of the great wheel of constellations, marked the passage of time. After each job that had taken me to a school—either nearby or in a faraway town—Elly and I traveled homeward with an appreciative longing for the quiet of our meadow.

It was often dark when we reached the dead end of our road and I performed the usual four-step ritual that

I always savored: open the gate, drive through, get out to close the gate, and drive back to the meadow. Always, during this coming-home ceremony, the metaphorical significance of the gate registered in my mind. It was like the hole down which Alice followed the rabbit or the door to H. G. Wells's time machine. The tipi in the meadow waited on the other side, and I never lost the privileged feeling of returning to a better place and time.

Elly always hopped out at the gate, serving as my Sacajawea for the final half mile. Loping in the bright cone of my headlights, she led the way. Confident and purposeful, she broke out into the great openness of the meadow as if she were leading a surprise attack on unseen intruders. Upon each return I cut the lights and let the truck coast softly over the grass under the silent stars. This muted return adjusted the senses, an acknowledgment to the gift of what we had here on the backbone of the mountain.

The dark shapes of deer often floated over the grass and melded with the black border of forest that bled outward into the unending mountain-scape. Elly gave chase like a lone, silent rocket but then circled back in admission that her predatory dash had only been for show. If the moon was up, the dip and swell of the meadow glowed like a great rolling sea, its waves frozen in their muscular pulsing. That final massive swale of grass before the ridge always dwarfed me and erased any sense of dominion I might entertain over this land. It set me alongside the field mouse that had invaded my granola, the cricket that sang in the dark, and the nighthawk that soared overhead at dusk. We all lived here. I was no less important, nor was I more.

I engaged the truck's gears for the final climb up to the far ridge, where the tipi loomed on the high point like an arrowhead, capping the land at the rim of the gorge that opened to the river far below. My home, a black starless point, jutted into the same black of the star-studded sky. Cutting off the engine gave the secret password that welcomed me back. The silence cleansed my ears. What had been posing as silence slowly revealed itself as the distant static of the river rising from the valley.

Sometimes I lay in the grass and gazed up into the universe, but Elly never could postpone her obligatory investigation of the area around the tipi. As it is with all sensible dogs, vigilance was a part of her job description. She checked for the scent of trespassers: fox, coyote, raccoon, or human. Watching her sniff her way around camp, I sometimes felt the need to explain to her exactly why we had left the meadow again for several days, but eventually I took it on faith that she had some understanding about *my* job description. After all, she went to the engagements and into the schools with me.

In those days, that was possible. Only a few times did a principal look into Elly's eyes and deny her entry. After the initial thrill of children welcoming her into their classroom, the excitement leveled off, and she politely curled up in a back corner to wait out my presentation. She never interrupted, but I can't claim the same courtesy for myself. Sometimes I used her as a teaching aid to illustrate the fine points of predator anatomy or animal gaits. She stood or walked in ladylike fashion and cut her eyes to me with a familiar question: *Can we go now?*

It was, I believe, a reasonable price to pay for living with me, and she tolerated it well enough. The kids, of course, loved her, always the first step toward accepting me. After all, how bad could a guy be if he took his dog to work?

Once a month I hosted outdoor weekend workshops for adults, with classes on plant foods and medicines, fire-making, stalking, tracking, hide tanning, bow making, and a gauntlet of survival skills.

Preparing for these workshops meant accumulating supplies and materials that my students needed. Because of my propensity to scavenge and because I felt as though I were sidling effortlessly through portals of time on each occasion that I left the meadow, I began to place more importance on rummaging through trash heaps. In fact, I made a game of it to see if I could find what I needed along the road before I resorted to purchasing it in a store. There has always been a special place in my heart for finding useful things that others have thrown away.

Knowing this, my friends weren't surprised to spot my truck pulled off the side of the road while I picked up a dead woodchuck or coyote. Collecting fresh roadkill offered a good way to study anatomy and specifically foot structure for tracking. The habit also kept me well stocked with skins to tan and to make into crafts. One of Teresa's friends nicknamed my truck, and the moniker stuck instantly: "the Buzzard Buggy." But there were more items on my list than just the corpses of unfortunate highway accidents.

My need for materials gave my Atlanta jobs new meaning because a generous network of streets—a neighborhood of the very wealthy—always offered the unexpected. On any other street curb in the sprawl of Atlanta, these castaway items would have sported price tags. Each time I traveled to the Buckhead section, I made a point to cruise the street-side trash piles of the rich and recycle-less. The experience never failed to be extraordinary—and it was fun, like a treasure hunt. I just had to be flexible about the treasures.

A one-day sample: a cord of cut and split hardwood stacked impeccably on the curb, a wooden crate, a shovel blade in need of a handle, a set of dusty glass storage jars with rubber gaskets and clampdown lids, a few pristine shelving boards, an old cast-iron frying pan begging for steel wool and elbow grease. More than a few times, I caught myself whistling an airy, familiar tune under my breath— on automatic pilot, so to speak. When the lyrics caught up to the melody, I realized I was happily mumbling "My Favorite Things." Once I actually came across a cardboard box filled—believe it or not—with broken-up kindling, bundled and tied with string. On other occasions I picked up two plastic crates from Mathis Dairy, another half-cord of firewood, and a retired set of perfectly good kitchen knives.

I felt like a time-traveler cheating history by slipping into the future to bring back tools before their time, but I did impose two rules on my finds, arbitrary though they were. I passed up an armchair, a desk, and a massive roll of unused carpet—anything not migratory or burnable. Even a thief of time must have standards.

In front of one estate—cattycornered from the governor's mansion—lay a huge dismantled wooden crate that might have housed a refrigerator or a vault. Two of the pieces were as big as a door and shored up by two-by-four bracing. Stenciled in black across the plywood facing were the words: "U.S. Ambassador to India."

This is what I mean by saying that I had to be flexible. I hadn't been thinking about a bed support, but I did prefer a perfectly flat and hard bed. I have no idea how that crate got there or if an international diplomat lived at that address. Nevertheless, that was how I acquired my authentic Indian bed for my tipi. The Trash Fairy was being very good to me. And clever.

Back in the mountains, I blocked one of the crate's plywood slabs off the ground with rocks, shimmed it level, and laid out my bedding on it. With winter fast approaching, a raised platform held an additional benefit besides the orthopedic needs for my spine. I would be warmer elevated from the cold ground, if only by a few inches.

Once I had installed it, I stared at the rigid rectangle of plywood and . . . began to have second thoughts. A nineteenth-century Native American had commented on the white man's proclivity for separating himself from the earth with chairs and beds. In ancient Greek myth, the giant Antaeus remained invincible as long as he maintained contact with the Earth. In one of his labors, Hercules cleverly lifted him off the ground and crushed him to death.

I weighed these considerations carefully, but what kept coming back to me was that we spend a third of our lives in a bed. To a large degree, the quality of the other two-thirds hinges upon how well we sleep through the bedtime third. I decided to keep the bed.

Around this bed and the place claimed by firewood, my living space began to take shape. The floor plan of a tipi is not a true circle, but it's close. Objects with right angles don't quite fit snugly into the scheme. They jut here and there and take up more space than they should. But everything I had found for creating vertical space was cubic: milk crates, shelving boards, the bed. The jars were about the only item with a rounded shape, but, by the time my home had settled into its finished decor, I considered the tipi's interior a unique blend of history, bricolage, and bric-a-brac. Paiute meets Picasso.

A tipi, by design, slants backward a bit, putting the entrance on the least-steep face of the asymmetrical cone. A rare show of angles covers the oval doorway—a rectangular flap of canvas stiffened by two wooden stays, like two curtain rods, one for hanging, the other for weighting. I carved mine from maple. The stays slipped into sleeves, both horizontal, one at the top, the other at the bottom of the door flap. The weight and stiffness of the stays gave the flap enough rigidity to seal the doorway adequately, though in high winds it was necessary to tie the bottom stay to the two nearest poles.

With a little time, the floor plan settled into a working arrangement with a pleasing, coincidental decor. Behind the door flap lay a personalized world of comfort and pragmatism. In winter, with a fire licking up from the pit, a tipi embodies coziness. There should be a better word for it because the ambience transcends anyone's notion of coziness. "Cozy" is like "cute." Both words gambol off the tongue, never conveying anything serious. My tipi space deserved more. It was . . . *nurturing*.

I had been sleeping in blankets donated by friends, but fall was ending, and winter was closing in. John Barbour, a friend who managed the outfitter store for the Nantahala Outdoor Center, had driven down from North Carolina, bringing me a sleeping bag along with a sheath knife, life jacket, canoe paddle, and rain suit for river trips. John was my Santa-come-early that first winter after the fire.

The fiber-filled coat I was wearing came from Cal Watford, owner of Call of the Wild, an outfitter shop near the summer camp. As I often did, I had stopped by to leave flyers for my workshops. Cal had heard about the fire. He led me over to a rack of jackets on sale and looked at me with a no-nonsense glare.

"Pick one out, and don't say a word," he instructed.

I started to utter something awkward, and he turned on his heel, leaving me in the company of strange garments hanging in a line, one insistently waiting to embrace me. It was like picking out a puppy at the pound—although I think in this case I was the puppy.

At the head of my bed sat one of the castaway Mathis Dairy milk crates set on its side to form a cubbyhole/bedside table. Inside it lay: the book I was reading; a box of matches; a notebook and pen with which I had begun to resurrect my novel from the ashes; a flashlight; a water bottle; a toothbrush and toothpaste; several small plastic film canisters for salt, pepper, and peppermint soap; and a sun-bleached turtle shell that held loose items like lip balm, coins, plumber's candles, and newly found arrowheads and other gems slipped into my pocket while walking in the forest. On top of the crate was a candle standing erect on a saucer-shaped stone, fixed in a hardened pool of its own melted wax.

Moving clockwise around the floor, my mouse-proof jars of rice, oats, and granola made a pleasant culinary sight. (The stones of the food cairn had been donated to my fire ring.) Next was my cookware: one donated saucepan with handle, another without that doubled as a bowl; the found frying pan, now rust-free and seasoned with oil; a plastic bag containing a sponge and a steel wool pad; one of the kitchen knives from the set I'd found in Atlanta; and my one eating utensil, which to this day I still prefer at all meals, civilized or not: a spoon. From the summer camp's lost and found, I'd salvaged a couple of towels. One stayed folded with these kitchen goods. The other, my bath towel, hung from the tipi's liner to dry.

In front of this kitchen space, within an arm's reach of the bed, lay a small pile of sticks varying in thickness from piccolo to oboe. This was my immediate supply of firewood, which I prepared on a nightly basis. Before retiring for a night, I would beef it up with several French horns and a couple of tubas.

Next around the perimeter came the long-term stack of firewood. This cache—more than any other possession in the winter months—defined my natural wealth. Whenever this pile of dry, sheltered wood began to dwindle, my own sense of security slid down the same curve. I was vigilant about it; some might say obsessed. I don't think the bottom half of any stack was burned but a few times. Nothing else was so acutely wired into the cause-and-effect territory of my consciousness.

If in early evening a winter storm swept into my meadow and if I was not prepared, I had to gear up and gather wet wood in the dark, appreciably delaying a hot meal in my dry living space. It was simple accountability in its clearest definition. No firewood = no fire = no warmth = a cold meal = a miserable experience.

Take notice, psychologists and psychiatrists who counsel the troubled teens of the world, those mired in complacency. I give you this new therapy regimen to prescribe at will: Erect a tipi in the patient's backyard in winter, and banish the teen from the house for the cold months.

Nothing felt as productive or as satisfying as collecting wood. Gathering sticks, breaking them into unique pieces to handle again in the middle of the night, stacking them—every step contained a grace and gratitude that went beyond what you might expect. The forest becomes like a bank with its vault doors thrown open to the public. The value of simple things—like sticks—skyrockets.

My primary firewood pile usually occupied a two-foot high by two-foot wide by five-foot long space at the three o'clock position of the floor plan, the door being at six o'clock. That stack of wood, my most valued possession, defined my wealth, and yet my door always remained unlocked. Oddly enough, if anyone had ever burgled me—which no one did—my firewood would probably have gone untouched.

On either side of the door, I intentionally kept nothing. This was the place most likely to get wet during a rainstorm after all, and sometimes it was utterly unavoidable. The leakage came not from the door but from the smoke hole above. The smoke flaps could be adjusted by their outside poles until both flaps angled far over to one side like neighboring vertical blinds. Through this position, smoke could still escape, and rain didn't enter. However, if the rain fell hard enough, that flap configuration could never completely shut out the invasion of wetness.

It was possible, though, to crisscross the flaps against the tipi and virtually seal out rain, like coat lapels flattened against the chest. The hole through which the poles protruded—analogous to the neck-hole of the coat—couldn't be perfectly blocked by the convergence of poles. Water entering there rode the smooth underside of each pole all the way to the ground.

But complicating the situation was that when the flaps overlapped to shut out rain, there could be no fire;

smoke had no way to exit. So it followed that rain always entered the living experience inside a tipi. With each heavy storm, there was a decision to make: drier tipi and no fire . . . or wet entranceway and warm fire. I almost always opted for the latter. I didn't mind sharing the front of my lodge with rain. It became a good place to store canned goods, which contributed some interesting counterpoint harmonies to the water thrumming on the canvas.

Counterclockwise from my bed, at the nine o'clock position, sat the other milk crate with perishables like butter, milk, and vegetables. This crate went outside when I cranked up the fire. Which brings us to one of the great advantages of tipi-life in winter. It's the complete opposite from the way we handle winter in houses. Have you ever thought how strange it is that we expend energy to heat up a large space, our apartments and houses, then expend yet *more* energy to run a cooling system in a small box in a room inside that large, heated space? A tipi sits inside the great refrigerator of the season. You only have to take a step away from the cover to store your perishables. I arranged my food on the ground and lowered the inverted milk crate over it like a cage, setting a large stone atop that. The cache was safe from everything but bears. But, I reasoned, if bears read the same books I did, they knew they were supposed to be sleeping through the cold months. And such was the case.

To play it safe, however, I did leave my scent of ownership. Each night, as a deterrent and a warning, I urinated in a circle around the food cache. This had worked on Georgia's barrier islands—Cumberland, Sapelo, and Ossabaw—where raccoon marauders were so plentiful that they fought one another for the right to a garbage bag that I'd hung from a tree limb. In those instances, I'd circled the tree trunk backward leaving a ring of repellant. It worked like an olfactory force field. Disgruntled, all the raccoons simply left, and I slept without further ado. From that tried and true experience, I reenacted the ritual there outside the tipi, laying down the gauntlet for the mountain critters as well. The message was tacit but clear:

Hear me, creatures of forest and field. This food is mine. Don't make me have to come out here and pee on you.

What if an anthropologist had been hiding in the laurels, studying me? Imagine his notes: My subject, Homo tipius, on the coldest nights erects a small food totem outside his lodge and balances a rock on top. Then, in a reverse gait, he carefully encircles the shrine, emptying his bladder to create a perfect yellow ring in the snow. This enigmatic ceremony may be intended to pay homage to Saturn or a piece of it that might have fallen to Earth here—hence, the rock. But why perform the rite walking backward? More data needed.

At the foot of my bed lay two stringed instruments: my guitar and a bow borrowed from camp. I was eager to make some new arrows so that I could return archery to my list of workshops. A few days after I had settled into my new home, I noticed someone walking toward me in the distance across the meadow. He carried a slender box. As he grew closer, I recognized a former archery student with a big smile on his face. He had brought me a set of matched arrows that he'd made in his workshop.

Around the lower half of the tipi's interior hangs a curtain of canvas called the liner, which is suspended from a rope that runs like a polygonal clothesline around the poles. This rope encircles each pole to prevent slippage. At each turn of the rope, two sticks are jammed parallel between rope and pole to allow an unobstructed path for the rainwater that trickles down the underside of the pole.

The liner serves three purposes, each borne out by the trial and error of historical practicality. Native Americans discovered that this extra layer made the tipi warmer in winter, especially since it fell all the way to the ground, where it lay as a flat ten-inch flange. This shut out any cool draft beneath the cover, which, you will remember, intentionally stands above the ground by a few inches.

The liner also afforded families some privacy. A tipi without a liner is a shadow show of grotesquely distorted silhouettes. In a village, such a tipi would make gossipy late-night viewing for the rest of the tribe. The original drive-in movie, if you like. There is also a story of a Plains native who, for some reason, lived without a liner one winter. An enemy shot at his shadow through the wall of his tipi and killed him. On the tribe's winter count—a spiral of paintings to mark each year with a memorable incident—this murder was recorded as the defining event of the year. Imagine curtains making the front page of the *New York Times*.

Most important, though, the liner creates an upward draft that carries smoke to and out the smoke hole between the flaps near the top of the cone. Since the liner is sealed to the ground and the cover is raised above the earth, together they work as a baffle. Remove the liner from a tipi, and woodsmoke wanders around aimlessly as though it can't find an exit.

Part of the close-at-hand pile of firewood nearest my bed always contained sticks of tulip magnolia, a light, porous wood that burns hot and fast. I called it "driving wood" and learned that it is a boon to a tipi dweller. Sometimes at night while I was asleep, even with the liner in place, the fire might lose its vitality and reduce itself to a serious smoker. Being only a few inches off the ground, I believed there was no need to fear asphyxiating, but a smoke-filled tipi is rough on the sinuses, and when the fire balked, the tipi, of course, got cold.

"Driving wood" quickly remedied the problem. I laid the sticks on the coals, blew them into flame, and the increased heat drove the smoke up and out of the tipi in seconds. Sometimes, if smoke had backed down from the tip of the cone too much, I stretched across my bed and stuck my face out the back of my abode, sliding one cheek along the ground and the other under the liner and cover to take in a blessed dose of fresh, cool air.

One cold December night, I awoke in a suffocating cloud of smoke—so thick that my body acted not out of conscious thought but by reflex. I couldn't see a thing as I plunged my face out the back, lifting the liner as I had done dozens of times before—only this time I was moving at the speed of survival. Apparently I awoke because my last sleeping breath had drawn in a heavy dose of acrid smoke. My throat and lungs were burning.

As I squirmed and stretched for a breath of fresh air, something slapped against my entire face and stung me from brow to chin. Still, I couldn't breathe. It was confusing. There was some obstacle in the way, and it had conformed to my skin like a mask. At that breathless moment, I didn't care if the rear end of a wooly mammoth had snuggled up to the back of my lodge—*I needed air.* Desperate, I rammed a hand ahead of my face to push away anything that might have nestled there. My lungs were on fire.

My hand plowed smoothly through the obstruction with a squeaking sound, and my fingers wriggled free into the night. A current of cool air rushed to my face, and I inhaled deeply several times. When I opened my watering eyes, I could make out a faintly luminescent glow, and a crusty clump of crystals fell from my nose.

It had snowed.

With a deep reserve of fresh air held in my lungs, I turned back to the smoky tipi and fumbled with my clothes until I had to return for another gulp of clean air. I repeated this several times. Finally bundled up and booted, I stepped out the doorway into the slow and silent drift of biscuit-sized flakes fluttering from a soft gray ceiling of clouds. The meadow was blanketed in a quilt of white, radiating a cool incandescent aura of quiet resolve.

I took a few steps and smiled at the snow's flawless stealth. It had arrived in total secrecy and had already sculpted the earth with a smooth and elegant four-inch coat. The tipi looked as though it fit into the landscape like a natural landmark that had grown out of the white, its base flared on a curve like concurrent roots tapping into the ground. The arc of snow had climbed gently up its slope where flakes had tumbled soundlessly down the canvas, sealing the opening at the bottom of the cover.

Using a long stick, I dug a trench around the perimeter of the tipi until smoke swirled out the top like gossamer ghosts of birds released from a grave. Imagine the old trick of raising a full drinking straw from a glass of water, lifting your finger, and watching the water flow down—only in this case the principle turned on its head. It was between 2 and 3 a.m. Standing in the middle of that pristine scene in the middle of the night, I wondered if anyone else in the mountains knew at that exact moment that north Georgia lay covered in snow.

After sealing myself back inside, I sat on the bed and looked at the fire that, now cleared of the backed-up smoke, had combusted back into flame. I took off my boots and thought about the seriousness of what had just happened. What if I hadn't awakened? Wasn't this the way that so many people died in house fires?—by smoke inhalation? Lifting the liner I checked the condition of the trough I had dug. Fresh flakes were already accumulating—beginning to fill up my air intake source again. Death by conspiracy between snow and smoke: a strange alliance. My internal alarm, fired by a survival instinct, woke me about every hour so I could reassess my home's status.

Now it was "cozy" with an edge, "nurturing" with accountability. I dreamed that night of a PVC pipe on a double angle, periscope-style. It fit under my liner and cover, delivering fresh air at all times to my face. I never resorted to such a contraption, but what had the Native Americans done about it? I never came up with much of an answer except that my three separate circumnavigations around the tipi with a stick that night were probably both historic and authentic. On that third trip outside, I was feeling pretty close to some nameless Cheyenne in the Nebraska Territory of yesteryear . . . and betting it was a woman.

11

Next to Godliness

How do you get yourself clean out here?"
One student from each of my workshops always
asked this question—especially in the winter months. The
river, within earshot of my home, was the obvious answer,
but people wanted to know details. The Etowah, like all
mountain streams, is *cold*—even in summer. Sit in it long
enough on a July afternoon and your lips will turn blue. A
little longer and you could experience the life-threatening
oxymoron of summer hypothermia.

Winter is another story entirely.

For river bathers in northern Georgia, a day comes in
November that tests for hardiness. The water temperature

drops to that unforgettable threshold that compresses the air in your lungs upon submerging. The gasp is involuntary. Like all physical discomforts, it's how you deal with it mentally that really counts. That first day of feeling the breath stolen from your lungs is a harbinger. You know that you're going to be repeating this stoic exercise for the next four months, come rain, shine, wind, or blizzard.

It was my entrenched habit, whenever possible, to get clean before I retired for the night. I slept better. Especially in a primitive situation—like one of my self-imposed survival trips, which I had been practicing for many years. On those excursions, a lot of work went into preparing a shelter. With that kind of labor comes sweat, oil, and grime, which leaves moisture on the skin's surface. If not removed, this liquid evaporates through the night, stealing energy from the body in the form of heat to make the leap from liquid to gas. Even in the summer in the mountains, that transfer could make for a long and miserable night. That kind of heat loss in winter could prove fatal.

There's a simple trick to staying warm at night. The equation consists of three parts: a lasting fire, a well-built shelter with plenty of insulation from the ground, and a bath. If you are fortunate enough to have a towel in a cold-weather survival situation, you could bypass the fire-building and appreciate the inestimable value of cloth as a water transfer device, body to towel, towel to air. Without that towel, a fire is a necessity—but not just any fire. It has to be reliable.

In tipi-life, I used both a fire and a towel. I brought my towel and mint soap to the river. At my bathing spot, I kept a bucket—one of those ubiquitous tall white plastic containers you can find abandoned in vacant lots across America. These are the containers that originally held ice cream, caulking compound, pool chlorine, or a hundred other commodities. I found mine, appropriately enough, at the edge of the river, probably jetsam tumbled from a capsized canoe somewhere upstream because one of those white buckets makes a pretty good dry-storage container for spare clothes.

At bath time, the first order of business was to build what I called a "surefire fire," one that would build steadily so that, by the time I returned, dripping cold from the water, the flames would be dependably welcoming. With the pyre lighted, I stripped down and draped my clothes on crude drying racks near—but not too near—the flames, so the fire could drive from the clothes the day's buildup of moisture.

Bucket in hand, I eased out into the river, careful not to stir up bottom silt. When the water reached my thighs, I lowered myself below the surface, scrubbed my scalp with my fingernails, and ran my palms all over my body to force water to mix with the impurities on my skin. On the way back to shore, I filled the bucket and climbed to the floodplain, where I lathered with biodegradable soap about fifty yards from the river's edge, this for the river's sake. "Biodegradable" soap does not biodegrade in water. To break down, it must contact the soil and its thousands of species of bacteria.

First, I lathered up my hair like whipped egg whites, my head then serving as my soap dish. My hands returned to my hair whenever I needed more suds for the rest of my body. Next a military press with the full bucket above my head and the initial rinse. Then, virtually soap-free, I returned to the river for a final submersion.

Because walking out of a river onto a Georgia floodplain is often a sandy or muddy proposition, I found a rock perch that acted as a stone bath mat for drying off. Depending on how much rain we'd had, my rock usually showed above the water about the size of an unabridged dictionary. It was just a jump away from dry land.

I returned to my fire with my towel and dried off every part of me except the bottoms of my feet. Next I donned T-shirt, shirt, and sweater. I stuffed a sock into each boot, tied one lace from each shoe together, and draped my footwear around my neck. Then I forked my pant legs around my neck over the boots, so that the legs hung down in front like wide suspenders. Over the pants I yoked my towel around my neck.

So draped, and with the order of my stacked clothing correct, I returned to the river, swished my feet in the water, and stepped onto my "changing rock." It was at this point that I always imagined being watched by a beaver or an otter. I must have looked like the Hunchback of the Etowah. If a human had seen me, an Appalachian legend could have been born—perhaps something to balance out Sasquatch in the Northwest.

Thus began the final ritual of dressing and drying. More than its exacting demands of laying out clothes in a logically sequential order, there was the crucial need for balance. For your consideration and posterity's sake, here's the formula:

Steady yourself on your left leg as you raise your right. With the towel, dry your right foot, then return the towel to its yoke position around your neck.

Root for the sock in your right boot, put it on, slip your pants out from under the towel, and fold each pant leg at the knee, pinching each cuff against the same side pocket.

Holding the doubled-up trousers as low as possible— without dipping them into the water, of course—point your right foot into the right pant leg and then, releasing the pinch on that cuff, extend your foot forward swiftly, like a fencer's thrust.

The timing of pushing your foot through its pant leg is vital. Too fast, and the fold in the material might not relax to allow passage of your foot. Such an unexpected short-sheeting of a pant leg can, by Newton's third law, send you and your dry clothes back into the river. Too slow, and the freed cuff will swing down to drag in the water. Done just right, you stand balanced with your right leg dry, covered, and pointing forward. At this moment you should closely resemble Rudolf Nureyev frozen in time during a performance. Tug the pants high on the waist, encouraging the pants to cling to your hips. At this point, your pants are half-on.

Next, tuck the left pant leg into the waist of the pants, slip the bootlace knot, and set the left boot on the rock next to your left foot.

Put on the right boot, tie the laces, and lower your dressed right foot to the rock.

Repeat the process in mirror image for the left side.

My perfect record in perched dressing comes from all the time I have spent stalking animals. Stalking requires and builds confidence in balance. In fact, I suggest this dressing-on-a-rock exercise to students of my stalking classes because the process is a full seminar on balance and accountability. A mistake—any lapse in concentration or judgment—might be costly, depending on the day's temperature . . . and whether you can make the emergency leap to shore. But my successes, I believe, prove that you balance better when you have a reason to be serious about it. Just the same, I always kept my jacket back on the floodplain near that waiting fire.

On January 1, in that first winter season of my tipi-life, the Etowah froze from bank to bank on those stretches of river that ran east to west or vice versa. Those sections never saw the winter sun, which arced low in the southern sky, hidden from the river corridor by mountain ridges and evergreen trees on the floodplain.

It was New Year's morning; so much of America was recovering from a wild night. My idea for New Year's craziness was to build a "white man's fire" on the floodplain and hit the river. I wanted to enter the New Year as clean and shining as a baby beaver's first incisor. When the fire showed conviction, I walked naked through single-digit air, cracked through the river ice step by step until I was able to lower my body into the gelid water. I didn't have to worry about perch-dressing. The frozen earth was iron-hard. No loose specks of soil or sand stuck to the soles of my feet. I couldn't have pried up dirt with a crowbar.

So why not just build a fire and dry off your sweaty body with the radiant heat, without the torture of getting into arctic water? The grime and salts saturating our sweat don't evaporate with the water. That residue remains on the skin and provides hiding places where water can cling with tenacity. Nothing beats a bath.

Besides, wild bathing is one of the true badges of intimacy with nature. It tightens that bond for which all children of wilderness crave, no matter the age. In the old days, most natives greeted the dawn by immersing themselves in water every day of the year. To move through a January day inside a body cleansed by winter waters is like wearing a holy garment anointed and encrypted with secret acceptance. If life began in the primordial soup as scientists believe, perhaps we have to return to it—even when freezing cold—to understand our place in the world.

Elly, I should mention, never bathed voluntarily, nor did she look askance at me as I waded out into frigid waters to satisfy my comfort needs for sleeping. She knew without a doubt which of us was the animal more demanding of comfort.

In my defense, it is only fair to remind you that dogs don't sweat through their skin, only through their paws. How much moisture can be held by paws constantly abraded by soil, leaf litter, and stone? Besides, I'm not flexible enough to lick myself clean all over. Even if I was, I'm not sure that I'd want to.

~ 12 ~

Neighbors

With winter fully arrived, my tipi came into its own. In its way, it was like a hemlock tree: evergreen, still functioning, and undaunted amid so much dormancy.

Snow is not a permanent winter feature of the north Georgia mountains. It comes maybe half a dozen times, once or twice substantially, and it might last on the ground for four or five days before our fickle weather turns unseasonably warm. But due to its humid air, the South can be much colder than outsiders might imagine.

As the surroundings paled into January's starkness and the season's gray, my lodge became a nucleus of activity. Smoke constantly curled from the apex like a slow, steady breath. If I was away for a while, I banked the fire accordingly. To return home a day or two later to see smoke still rising above the poles was like spotting a warm yellow light glowing above a back porch, as if some loyal friend was waiting for me. On those nights of walking from river to meadow, seeing the fire still flickering through the canvas always made me stop and smile. If I didn't already live there, I would have wanted to.

Shards of broken wood lay scattered around the camp like mulch, each piece a memento of recent carving or splitting or sharpening for some craft or chore. The inevitable pathways that radiated from the door became the prologues to stories that described all the facets of my life. The path to the white pines for kindling or sap for making glue. The path to the hardwoods for more substantial firewood. The path to the river for a bath or to clean my cookware or to dig cattails or wapato or to hunt for crayfish. The path to my truck when I trekked off to a job. The path to the rock outcrop where I liked to lean back against a boulder, write, and gaze out into the vast valley that yawned above the serpentine course of the river.

The presence of the tipi deepened my sense of remoteness on the ridge because it reminded me constantly that I was not visiting but here to stay. Being so involved with this corner of the land—spending so much of my time in this one back pocket of the meadow—gradually introduced me to all those creatures that had staked a claim for themselves before I had arrived as a squatter.

Not twenty yards from the tipi, a gray fox sometimes skirted the edge of the clearing at twilight. Always he moved at a wary trot, but once or twice I witnessed him boldly crossing the open ground of the meadow grass under moonlight. After that first spotting, I kept a regular watch in the evenings.

I am somehow connected to foxes. I have no explanation for this. Whenever I have chanced to meet a fox in the wild, time has stopped for me—and something else strange has happened. My perspective expanded to include two views of the world. Not only did I see the fox and commit to memory every visual nuance of the sighting, but also I could see myself through the fox's eyes. I felt its experience as sharply as I felt my own. The encounter held me for days as though the mental footage running through my mind held an encrypted message for me to decipher.

One cold dawn, I laced on newly made moccasins, left Elly with strict instructions to stay (tied to a tree outside the tipi), and stalked the Etowah's floodplain just to see what I would see. The ground was like cold steel. The temperature had been hovering in the low teens for several nights, and the earth had clenched into a metallic fist, as though a heavy step might resound like the peal of an anvil struck by a hammer.

After an hour exploring the flood plain, I changed directions and stalked uphill, climbing above the sharp bite of humid air that pooled at the bottom of the valley. I kept my ascent slow, muscular, and fluid, grasping the earth with each step like the gentleness of a feather come to rest. Halfway up the slope I came face to face with a four-foot-long icicle clutching the overhang of a car-sized boulder. The frozen stalactite tapered to a point like a single great fang. The perfectly formed sculpture was bright and clean and dry as bone. I leaned close, touching it, closed my eyes, and inhaled the cold fire emanating from its surface.

Then something approached noisily from the far side of the rock. I stilled myself and waited.

A rabbit scrambled around the boulder, skidded to a stop at my feet, then veered off down the mountain in a frantic dash. Still, I didn't move. Ten seconds passed. Then a more subtle rhythm broke the silence that had gathered around me. It poured along the rabbit's trail like a delayed wake. A gray fox rounded the rock at a steady, contained clip. Its demeanor seemed both casual and deliberate. Its body appeared to float down a rough staircase of jumbled stones that its prey had leapt. The descent was remarkable, the rufous-gray torso gliding like quicksilver across a tilted tabletop. The vulpine legs worked like finely calibrated shock absorbers making up every measured difference in the rugged terrain. Against this complicated adjustment of gait, the balletic smoothness of its upper body seemed impossible.

The fox came up to me as though I were invisible. This was my twilight fox, I knew—the animal I had come to know in profile. I was looking squarely into his face from two feet away. Something in its guileful eyes suggested that this was a male, verifying my earlier presumption.

I was gathered into a compact silhouette, my legs melded together, my arms drawn into the mass of my body, my head low to obscure the "fruit stalk" of my neck. I had calmly willed myself into a stump, a jut of rock, or an icicle. The fox slowed to a walk and passed me on the downhill side, strolling so close that, had I pivoted my left foot on its heel just an inch, the toe of my moccasin would have stroked the hairs of his left flank. The moment was strangely familiar, as though we met here on a regular basis. But the completeness of my anonymity, the remarkable intimacy of our rendezvous enraptured me.

As soon as he had passed, my gut told me that he was aware of his mistake, though he did not manifest it—a male non-gesture if ever there was one. He moved on in an insouciant trot, stopped at the next rock, and turned in profile, looking and listening down the hill for the rabbit. His eyes pointed down into the valley, but I was sure he was checking on me. I had the distinct feeling that he was embarrassed. If I had spoken, I was certain he would have despised me.

My eyes dissected every nuance of his posture. When he turned to leave, I knew I would forever recall his fluidity, his effortless pattern of placing a hind foot into a front-foot track, his gathered walk that set each foot down on the same thin line of his center of balance—like a tightrope walker. Then he dissolved into the forest without a sound. So empty and clueless was the scene after his departure that for a brief moment I questioned the reality of the experience. But the expansion of my spirit beneath my skin left no doubt. From that one private lesson of his talents, I became a better stalker, learning from a master, just as the Cherokee had centuries ago.

Many weeks later at twilight, two hundred yards from my tipi, I crawled on my belly through the desiccated meadow grass, settled in with my chin on the backs of my hands, and watched for an hour as a red fox hunted some elusive prey in a swatch of green grass. This fox stood rock-still with its haunches gathered and head held high, cocked to one side, its black ears erect. There was a subtle shift of energy that poured into the rear legs, and then suddenly it went airborne, the smoothest release of a spring I had ever witnessed.

At the apex—a good three feet above the earth—its body jackknifed with the grace and precision of a platform diver so that all four feet came together into an area no larger than my hand. The hunter hit the ground full of anticipation, but its head immediately pivoted to one side and froze again.

This fox must have been after a vole, but apparently the rodent had darted through a tunnel in the grass. The vole was smart: It froze, too. Had it kept running, the fox surely would have pinpointed its location. As it was, the fox wasn't sure. It waited, hoping for another telltale rustle in the dry grass.

Wait . . . listen . . . gather . . . spring—pounce—freeze. Repeat.

What must the drama be like from the meadow mouse's viewpoint? To think that a predator a hundred times its size was hovering over it like a cunning and methodical flyswatter. All the vole knew was its tunnel system. That and the inherited wisdom of speed, hiding, stillness, and silence. How did it know when to bolt? Did it trigger off the first delicate snap of grass blades as the fox touched down? Or was it the takeoff? Probably the takeoff. Sometime before the fox had hit terra firma, it was already turning its head—trying to track the vole's new hiding position.

It was a dance with death, hunter and hunted, nourishment and starvation. There are always two sides— two ends to the same string of life. Neither is right or good or favored. It is a relationship. We should celebrate not the outcome but rather the balance. The fox failed, but it would return. The fox would improve—or die of hunger trying.

When the fox finally would make its kill, the vole would fuel the turning of the great wheel of life. Four new field mice would take the vole's place. It is why meadow mice enjoy such prolific rates of reproduction.

There are always two sides.

~ 13 ~

Medicine Bow

It had been the summer of 1978 when Elly and I first moved to the mountains to stay. Twenty miles outside the small gold-mining town of Dahlonega I'd built an arched shelter in a remote part of the national forest, and there we slept each night. During the day I studied maps at the courthouse and called on landowners about the possibility of selling a choice parcel of their property. These were long days with little to show for my efforts except a better knowledge of Lumpkin County.

After three weeks of catching on average one copperhead every other night at our campsite, I decided not to press my luck any more. I was obviously near a den of vipers; no matter how many times I transplanted captured serpents to distant areas, the supply from the den might be endless. It was only a matter of time before I would roll over on one in the dark.

As if to support that warning, one late afternoon, returning to my shelter after a three-day absence, I stooped to enter and was attacked by a swarm of cicada-killers that had taken up in what they must have seen as the wasp hangar of their dreams. The first sting caught me on the brow above my right eye and carried the wallop of a baseball bat in the hands of an angry five-year-old. This was the first in a string of eviction notices I would receive in the mountains. Not having enough daylight to construct another shelter, I raised the white flag that evening and unrolled my bedding under the stars with the copperheads. Wasps, diurnal, sleep at night, so when clouds blotted out the constellations, I stalked inside to my old bed under its roof. The next day Elly and I moved on, looking for less venomous environs, I trying to appear as dignified as possible with my new lopsided forehead. It was the face only a mother or a man's dog could love.

We crossed the watershed to the north and rented an unheated attic in the house of an elderly couple on Suches Creek. When I first talked to my future landlords about living with them, they kept their smiling eyes on Elly and asked me all about her. They were clearly dog lovers. I don't remember them asking a single question about me. Elly got the room, and they let me stay there with her.

Courthouse research had proved fruitless and tiresome. On days when I didn't have a job working as a naturalist, Elly and I drove the back roads and looked for land to buy. On lesser-traveled dirt roads, we developed a ritual. I stopped, reached across, and opened her door. She climbed out to the real-time, undiluted world of foot travel and ran ahead of the truck like my flagship. This must have done wonders for her self-esteem. My pathfinder, she was forging a way to our future home—unless a deer bolted across the road. When that happened, all canine allegiance to the land search, to me, and to that night's meal dissolved instantaneously. Everyone has a weakness. That was hers—testing her speed against a deer's.

On three occasions I had to segue from a land search to a dog search. Each time, she remained missing for several days. Each time we found each other, there was a lot of whining, licking, and wasted lecturing about getting lost.

Although it was a positive step to be finally living in the mountains, Mr. and Mrs. Landlord went through multiple packs of cigarettes a day. As I slept, I dreamed I was a slab of beef hanging in their smokehouse. When winter came, the attic took on arctic conditions. The downstairs windows were closed against the season, and the secondary smoke became unbearable. I approached my landlords about the problem. They became incensed and asked me to leave on the spot. In retrospect, it would have been smarter to have Elly broach the subject with them. Maybe a note tied to her collar written in block letters with my left foot:

DEER FOKES,

TABACKA SMOKE IZ BAD FUR DOGZ.

MAY BEE YOU KOOD PUFF OUTSIDE AND

DOWNWYND.

LUV, ELLY

It's always easier to think of the smart thing in hindsight.

The landlords were transplants from Florida, so I didn't consider my eviction a rebuff from the mountains. Actually, in most Appalachian circles, a Floridian ouster might be a badge of honor on one's résumé. Those Florida snowbirds crowded the mountains and drove up land prices and taxes. As unexpected changes often do, being banned from Suches Creek led to better things.

Elly and I migrated south over the mountain, back toward Dahlonega. First evicted by snakes and killer bees, and now, albeit the smolder of a cigarette, by fire—the latter to become a recurring theme.

That was a cold winter, and I needed somewhere to base, to build a fire at night, while I continued to look for land and teach nature classes. Ben and Dana, outfitters in Dahlonega who catered to Appalachian Trail hikers, came to my rescue. It was they who later lent me the tent after the house fire. Already, we had become fast friends. Because they also ran a campground, they offered me their most remote and primitive campsite to establish my winter home—a site no one asked for in the coldest season. My abode was a three-sided log structure with a concrete floor and a lean-to, shake-roof. On that open side, I could have a fire.

I got to know Dahlonega through identifying acreage that appealed to my eye and to my teaching needs. That winter I tried a new approach, writing more than a hundred letters to absentee landowners and knocking on at least as many doors until I found a place I couldn't pass up. It wasn't for sale, but I could lease it for a nominal fee if I served as guardian over the land.

On more than a hundred acres of forest and field bordering the Etowah River, a turn-of-the-century, wood-frame farmhouse sat on the property where the dead-end road terminated at the property's gate.

Now I had a place for students to gather, to learn about nature and the survival skills of the Cherokee. I named my school Medicine Bow, after the Native Americans' ceremonial bow, one never used for killing but only for spiritual growth. I taught on this land for seven years, while again beginning a new spiral path of discovery. Each summer I returned to the old summer camp in the piedmont, and, as I had been doing for years, brought the more adventurous kids to my new place in the mountains—this time to my new residence. I was commuting again, but this time the direction for coming home was the right one.

In that last summer on the land, everything changed in one split second of unforeseeable violence. That life-changing lightning bolt destroyed virtually everything I owned. Again, fire had driven me from my home, and once again an unexpected change led to something better. A tipi.

A tipi is a perfect centerpiece for the sunburst of directions for exploring land. In fact the shape of the lodge suggests the hub of a great vortex of space. My tipi reminded me daily that I lived at the heart of a great spiral of possibilities, like a sun centered in its solar system. Unless I walked back toward the road to the site of my former house, there was nothing but miles of wilderness in every direction.

In ever-widening journeys I learned the land around me in ways that I hadn't while living in the house. The distance from the burned house to the ridge where I set up the tipi was only a half mile, but it seemed to extend through centuries. My attitude about the land evolved to something wholly different.

I no longer needed those self-imposed survival trips—the ones designed to employ all the skills that I had taught my students. In tipi-life, some part of every day required one or more of those skills. I was living it. There probably wasn't a school in the world that could have better prepared me for my life's work. Anything I needed to learn about wilderness lore, I could learn in tipi-life.

I had to.

14

Homeland

After my first year of tipi-life, I finally found the land that I wanted to buy as a permanent base for my wilderness school. I'd been searching for it for fifteen years. I was forty-two years old. It was time to compromise on one item, though: no river.

Leasing the land on the Etowah had, in a sense, spoiled me. I was going to miss the constant music sung by its wide ribbon of sliding water, its whispery conversation with stone. But at the new land there was a creek, a swamp, and a meadow; flat land, rolling hills, and steep mountain slopes. All of it suggested isolation, whether among hemlocks or hardwoods, fern beds or thickets. Bear, bobcat, cougar, coyote, deer, fox, hawks, owls, rabbits, raccoons, snakes—they all lived there. A wooded bowl of a valley provided the perfect spot for base camp.

A national forest bordered the land on three sides. There were no buildings, no neighboring houses to interfere with a feeling of remoteness. My new location lay ten miles outside Dahlonega, a quaint town with a quiet pace, so I was still within easy driving distance of the clientele I had accrued from my work in and around Atlanta.

I shook hands with the sellers, joining the ranks of the landed gentry, keeping watch over this new land of which I was now steward. A new Medicine Bow, a new spiral path to begin. But first, I had to get my tipi there.

There is no picture quite like seeing everything you own packed into a truck beneath the horizontal canopy of seventeen tipi poles lashed to a canoe rack. The collection of poles says: *You are complete, autonomous, nomadic.* So outfitted, I migrated north in my pickup travois from the south end of the county. South to north for the winter— historically backward yet again.

Perhaps the most antithetical aspect of this event, historically speaking, was Elly riding inside the truck with me. Remember, the first Plains people—before the Spaniards' reintroduction of horses to North America—used their dogs as beasts of burden. A dog dragged a pair of slender tipi poles crossed over its back and lashed with crossbar slats to make a sled. Elly might have been able to drag one of these enormous poles slowly but certainly not with any gear attached to it. It would have been less a sled than an anchor.

We drove through the town square of Dahlonega, primarily a tourist town that has seen just about everything. In the 1830s it was the site of a major gold rush, and the opportunists who flocked there wrought havoc on the land and its native inhabitants. In their frenetic scramble to amass as much property as possible and to make the big strike, the gold-fevered whites of European stock exhibited a pattern of behavior that repeated itself all over America: They drove out the people who most venerated the land, who knew it best—in this case, the Cherokee.

I wondered, as I made my brief appearance at the town square, carrying all my belongings—the most obvious being a full-sized Plains tipi: Did any passerby glance my way and consider that a quiet invasion was under way? Did some town loiterer rush inside a store and look with panic to the proprietor and exclaim, "Injuns! They're back!"

I had met a lot of people around the county, yet not one of them fit the stereotype of the get-rich-at-all-costs American land grabber. In fact, everyone with whom I had talked held the Cherokee in high regard.

These days the steady onslaught of travelers provides a parade of curious faces through the town: Harley bikers en masse, recreational vehicles that look like warehouses on wheels, SUVs with canoes, kayaks, and mountain bikes piled on top so high that you wonder if the boats and bikes are tied to the car or the other way around, tour buses that test the scale of our humble streets. In them, people from up north who talk with the lingual tension of a square knot and remind us that we talk with an unhurried slur.

Elly and I expanded on that theme. We must have looked like our own version of a parade. As we cruised away from the square, balancing seventeen skinned trees almost twice as long as the truck, several people took note. Outside the Farmer's Co-op, a weathered man in coveralls stood by his truck and peered at us through his pipe smoke.

His head turned as we passed, but he did not return my wave. *What now?* he must have wondered.

Ten miles northwest of town, we left the pavement. The sound of the dirt road under the tires softened into a prelude of anticipation. I stopped at the gate, got out, opened it, drove forward, and closed the gate—hearing the click of the latch both as a farewell and a greeting. Good-bye to the years of searching for and dreaming of land. I had grabbed mine with the lifetime of savings I had hoarded away.

"Welcome to Medicine Bow," I said to Elly.

When I coasted into the pasture, turned off the key, and listened to the last of the summer crickets in my new meadow, those haunting words attributed to Chief Seattle came rising from memory like the murmur of forgotten spirits hovering over the ground—

"How can a man own the earth?"

I stood with one foot in the truck for a while and tried to take it all in. "My land"—an unpracticed phrase new to my tongue—had become something solid underfoot. "My land" was dripping with colors, mapped by animal trails, nests, and signatures of hoof, claw, and talon. Collectively it sang of dynamics and balance. It contained everything I needed to know. My arrival felt like stumbling upon a great mystical tome that had been waiting here for me to find—one that could not possibly be read in a lifetime.

Elly stood in the passenger seat. Staring out the windshield, she shifted her weight from leg to leg, kneading the cushion. A current of anticipation hummed through her. I knew the feeling. She made a high keening sound deep in her throat and then flicked her eyes to me for permission. When I spoke, she leapt out the window.

Toward the alders the creek rippled over stones that the Cherokee had stepped upon. A red-shouldered hawk cried repeatedly from the tallest white pine beyond the creek. The great trees of the property stood as monuments to their own history. The steep rise and fall of the land surrounding the meadow spoke of an even more ancient story when the earth had buckled here in a great chain that eventually earned the melodic name of Appalachia, a word erroneously coined by a cartographer who confused the Cherokee with a tribe far to the south in the coastal plain.

"How can you buy or sell the sky, the warmth of the land?"

I had stroked my name in ink across the real estate contract and paid out the bulk of my life savings, but I didn't feel that I owned this land. Indeed, it was I who was owned, like an orphan newly adopted.

"If we sell you our land, you must remember to teach your children that the rivers are our brothers and yours, and you must henceforth give the rivers the kindness that you would give my brother."

I closed my eyes and took in a deep lungful of air. Tasting the sweet scents of this land, I tried to hold onto that breath, to immerse myself fully into the baptismal moment.

"If we do not own the freshness of the air and the sparkle of the water, how can you buy them?"

The land was omniscient, my new mentor. I, the initiate, wanted a permanent record of this transaction . . . something more than a piece of paper.

"Every shining pine needle, every sandy shore, every mist in the dark woods, every clear and humming insect is holy in the memory and experience of my people."

Would I die here?

"The white man's dead forget the country of their birth when they go to walk among the stars. Our dead never forget this beautiful Earth, for it is the mother of the red man. We are part of the Earth, and it is part of us."

The breath eased from my lungs. My ownership of that breath had passed. But I inhaled again to begin the process anew, knowing that life is measured in moments.

Stepping completely out of my truck, I experienced one of those ineffable, clarifying moments of shifted perspective. I imagined my body rising, climbing high enough to take in the bigger picture that so often eludes us. From that perch in the sky, I could see my earthly self as no larger than a leaf among a forest of leaves in a sprawling, verdant valley—one leaf among many, no more and no less important than any other.

For a time I would be privileged to call this place home, just as others had before me, and in a sense I would be spiraling back, metaphorically making a circle by bringing forward the old ways of the Native Americans, teaching others how to live them. The students who would come here would bestow an attentiveness to the land. The trees and the creatures would sense this, but how did that process work exactly? Would the clicking sound of working with stone or the scent of hides being tanned or the lightness of a stalker's step, would they awaken a forgotten memory for this land?

Elly trotted briskly across the meadow grass. She stopped and smelled something at her feet and then looked around. She moved more slowly in a half circle, sniffing, picking up from blades of grass signals that I could never fathom. If anyone owned this land, she did. But she owned the essence of wherever she was. She understood ownership without taking possession. It could have been Elly's words just as easily as Chief Seattle's.

"How can any man own the earth?"

"I don't know," I said aloud, and Elly looked at me as if she might show me.

I carried the poles along the floodplain by the creek two at a time—one on each shoulder. I walked slowly, constantly turning my head to absorb all I could. Ripe muscadines scattered underfoot. Some of the fall asters were blooming—the blue ones that appear to conceive a soft neon glow at dusk. The floodplain spread before me in a sea of green ferns: lady, cinnamon, hay-scented, New York, Christmas, royal, and maidenhair. Here the shoulders of the creek pooled with a dappling of springs fed by a wealth of water just underground. Tracks of gray fox made crisp prints in the soft sand by the water. Sycamore, black birch, hemlock, a grove of tulip trees, bloodroot and Indian cucumber, sassafras, and white pine.

When the trail fizzled out, I rounded the mountain and found the best route for getting the poles through the maze of trees. These first steps laid down the foundation of a trail for my future students as they arrived at my campground. My future was this nascent path, materializing in its own natural time. I was a bud opening in autumn. Everything here—plants, animals, talking waters, the sculpture of the land—all shaped what I would do and teach and be, just as it had shaped those before me.

Again, the tipi played its part. The length of the poles dictated the path I forged while carrying them. No sharp turns. Instead, my meanderings unfolded with economy. Already the path my students would take had been laid out by the influence of my abode.

In the bowl-like valley where the campground would be situated, I stopped and turned my head—imagining my tipi in half a dozen places. The freedom of that simple choice was both exacting and serendipitous. I had to be attentive to drainage and deadfalls. But there were aesthetics to consider as well. The tipi would adorn and improve any site that I considered, a powerful testimonial for a home.

When I pictured the tipi in the shadow of the two tallest hemlocks, I smiled, walked to that place and set down the first two poles. Fifteen to go. I walked quietly back to the truck. The need for reverential attentiveness measured every movement I made. Grace and fluidity filled me. Something abstract wrapped around me and followed wherever I went. It was ceremony—not initiated by me, but unsolicited, celebrating a marriage of man to land. We exchanged vows in silence. This land belonged to me only because I belonged to it. The tipi defined the equation.

Ceremony came that way to me sometimes, seeping into my day like a subtle dye that changed everything without the bias of intention or knowledge or guidance. On some days when I gathered wild foods, I would stop at a plant and pause to gather my thoughts of thanksgiving before speaking the words of the harvest; on other days I said nothing at all because I was living the thanks within every moment, within every movement. I was wrapped in suspended reverence—quiet and complete. This moving-in day was one of those.

The tipi served as my bridge from the old land to the new. In some ways my life hadn't changed at all in that migration because I was still living the tipi-life. In other ways my commitment to the land had permanently altered my life. Did the Plains Indians live with such a contradiction? They had probably experienced something else entirely because their culture was devoid of the concept of owning land. Their appreciation most likely distributed itself equally over all the lands that they called home.

By twilight I had packed in my gear, even carrying in the big reflector-stone that I couldn't part with. The tipi fit among the trees as though it had been missing there for centuries. It released something in the valley, as if its poles had penetrated deep into the earth and tapped into a trapped pocket of the past. From my first fire, smoke slid from the top of the cone down the slope of the canvas, hanging low to the ground like a gray snake spreading a message of my arrival. A low pressure system, which meant it would rain by morning, maybe sooner.

Back at the creek, I found my bathing spot for another fall and winter, spring and summer. The stream flowed out of the national forest, filtered through millions of leaves, cobbled by stones, and curried by sticks and fallen trees. It was as pristine as nature intended. I returned to the tipi clean and naked, my clothes bundled under my arm. I dried my hair by the fire. My integration had begun.

As I lay in bed and cataloged the new sounds around me, I now knew that something had been missing from my former site on the ridge. It was water. I had listened to the Etowah every night, but the sound came from a distance. The closer I slept to the heart of the earth, to its low ground where the streams ran, the closer I felt to the source of all life.

Perhaps I had known this intuitively as a boy, when I had followed creeks for miles simply to walk through a corridor rich with green growth. Maybe it was the pungency of the plants in a more humid setting, or maybe the barred owl had something to do with it on this night. Its call from the floodplain sounded an anthem to acceptance, a secret revealed, an unfolding of the heart of this forest.

The Cherokee saw the owl as a messenger of death. I did not. A screech owl and a great horned owl added their voices to this bowl of land where I would sleep, and I could think of no sweeter music—until the rain began to fall.

The droplets came intermittently at first, then pattered insistently on the canvas just inches above me as proof against the storm. I settled into my bed and listened, and it was enough simply to listen and be.

I was home.

15

A Spiral Path

In the forest, a path establishes itself by certain rules. For most animals, a route of passage needs to be safe, hidden, or offer a chance of food or water.

For humans, the priority of a sylvan route is usually a path of least resistance. Comfort rules us. This usually means the shortest, least meandering route from point A to point B. If a large branch breaks off a tree and falls across a footpath, requiring a hiker to either bend down or climb over, a looping side-detour almost always emerges, and the former segment of inconvenienced path will revert to pathlessness, thereby reshaping the trail. Embrace the falling branches: There are enough straight lines in this world.

Once established, paths sustain themselves by welcoming travel. When an animal encounters terrain through which it wishes to cross, if it sees a path, it takes it. Creatures of habit use them repeatedly until the soil beneath compacts so much that a seed might have difficulty germinating there. Even if it's a seed that prefers hard-packed soil, like plantain or mullein, the sprout hasn't much of a future under the hooves, paws, and boots that will tread upon it. Which also suggests how a path can become a rut.

There is another way to cover ground—an all-encompassing one. It is based upon a circle, a geometrical figure sacred to most cultures, including the Native Americans. They knew that the Maker of All Things employed the circle repeatedly in the architecture of creation. The sun and the moon are circles; both travel a circular path. A bird's nest demonstrates a circle, as does the hawk's ascent as it rises on a thermal. A persimmon that drops into still water broadcasts perfect concentric circles that expand into larger ones. The seasons circle . . . as do our lives.

The Native Americans believe that each person's life is a circle, complete even at birth. Time and growth simply enlarge it. The riddle of the Sphinx, from the mythology of ancient Greece, helps to verify this notion. We begin our existence in total dependence; then we crawl until we can walk upright, only to bend earthward again until we return to our original state of helplessness.

A spiral is a broken circle, slightly skewed, patiently seeking to expand itself. It was the natural paradigm for me, just as it is the calling of all thorough explorers. Moving along this path ensured that I missed nothing. Along this ever-expanding series of turns, I intersected all those routes that radiated from my starting point like the spokes of a wheel. In fact, from the spiral I could catch glimpses of the parts of the path I'd already left behind. I could draw comparisons, past to present. *What was I then? What am I now?*

As a child I followed this spiral pattern of exploration out of necessity—first learning the "wild" places closest to my home and slowly advancing outward in all directions along that unending arc. How else could I have done it? I was, after all, traveling by foot and driven by a curiosity about each of the cardinal directions and all hybrid vectors in between. It was a perfect way to begin, and as an adult it is still useful.

If I spin off my spiraled orbit and take a large leap, if I omit or move too fast, I always wonder what I missed. Straight lines have their place but never for too long. If I take a job in a distant state, step onto an airplane, and touch my feet back to Earth a thousand miles from home, at the core of me I feel utter disconnection, as if I have somehow cheated myself of earning the distance. If I fly far enough, I meet people who speak a different tongue, and the disjointedness of the journey turns it bathetic. To ground myself, all I know to do is to start spiraling again to learn this new place and perhaps think of it as another life, another beginning place.

From the moment that I had first staked my tipi to this new patch of earth, its site had pinpointed a new center for my spiraling life. It became the hub of my universe. Each evening, when I returned home from a day's excursion, I brought with me the experiences of that day and stored them alongside all the others of previous days.

But sometimes, life in a tipi develops into a surprise party. The crowning experience of the day was waiting inside the lodge, anticipating my return. On one such occasion at the end of summer, when I had spent the better part of a day with fourth graders roaming the forest, we marched back into camp, most of them tired and hungry. Many of these children were about to sleep out in the woods for their first time. As we talked about preparing our supper, their teacher and I began to see the first signs of homesickness and uncertainties about the coming night.

While it was still light, we gathered inside the tipi where twilight held permanently. I wanted to talk about how to feel comfortable in the woods at night, and I thought that the intimacy of the tipi would provide the proper ambience. We settled in, but I stalled; the students didn't yet seem ready to listen. Like all my visitors, they began looking around and asking questions about the tipi. Then, by chance, someone offered the perfect segue.

"Do you ever get scared sleeping out here all by yourself?"

It was a reasonable question from a ten-year-old who had little experience with the nocturnal world outside his home or away from his family.

"Well, first of all," I said, "what is there to be afraid of out here?"

"Bears!" someone blurted out, and no one laughed.

Without offering details for the public record, I thought back to my last bear confrontation around the tipi. "I've had plenty of encounters with bears in these woods. Some of those were at night. Each time we've met, the same thing happens. The bear looks at me with a startled expression, turns to bolt, and crashes through the woods like a runaway freight train."

"Were you scared?"

"The bear was scared. Remember, he was the one who ran."

After a beat of consideration: "What if he'd run like that right at you?"

I nodded at another fair question. "*If* that happened, I'd be scared," I said. "But it would be very rare for a black bear to behave like that." They were imagining me as a late night snack for a black bear. "But we learn through experience what to be afraid of. I've learned to respect bears but not be afraid of them."

"What about snakes?"

"I've been visited by snakes in the tipi."

"Did they bite you?"

I shook my head. "I was too big to eat."

"But what about poisonous snakes?"

"No venomous snakes have come inside. They seem to be more cautious of people, which is probably why they sometimes bite humans. They fear us. They know that *we* are dangerous."

"What did you do to the snakes that got in here?"

"I asked them to stay and eat the mice that come in here to raid my food."

Silence.

Some of them looked at the flimsy door that separated the interior of the tipi from the rest of the wild world. There probably wasn't an animal on Earth that couldn't breach my minimal security.

"So you're not afraid at night?"

I thought about my answer carefully. I couldn't talk down to them from the vantage point of age. I had to remember where they were in their evolution of getting comfortable with the world.

"We tend to fear what we don't understand. The *unknown* is what eats at us. Mysteries nag. They make us less sure about ourselves. The night, because it robs us of the luxury of identifying what is around us, disguises everything as a mystery. A simple pile of sticks outside the tipi is no longer a stash of firewood. It becomes a nest of things that bite or sting or screech. Our surroundings become a maze of ambushes. We are fumbling through a new world where our favorite sense fails us. The night becomes the unknown—until we get to know it better."

Their eyes grew wide. They began quiet exchanges between themselves, and those discourses seemed healthy, so I remained silent, watching them trying to reassure one another.

It was at that moment that I saw the snake, draped on the top of the liner rope across from me, just beside the door. I don't know how I'd missed it, even in the grainy light of the tipi. This black rat snake was easily six feet long and thick as my forearm, the largest of its kind I'd ever seen. It hung in heavy loops along the rope, a veritable festooning of sleek, reptilian muscle. My first thought was: *These kids are never gonna believe this wasn't a setup.*

I'd gotten to know this rat snake through the summer months—even picked it up a few times for an impromptu lesson on snake anatomy with students. Because of its size, this giant had always been spotted at a distance; now it was practically hovering on top of us, just a few inches above several of my young guests' heads. To anyone without snake-savvy, it looked to be waiting in ambush for the expressed purpose of devouring a tipi full of children.

My eyes didn't linger on the unexpected visitor. The last thing I wanted was for one of these children to spot it and panic. I pictured a cartoon frame with child-sized bulges ballooning in all directions from the tipi cover. No one would have gone near the door, where the giant serpent perched overhead.

Keeping my face neutral, I leaned toward the children and whispered, "If I tell you a really special secret, will you all promise that you will remain very quiet and very still so that you can think about it?" As I had spoken, the children reflexively leaned toward me in perfect mirror image, waiting.

Finally one of the more outspoken students shrugged, assuming proxy for the group in a flippant tone. "Sure."

I leaned even closer and slowly shook my head. "No . . . I mean *real-ly* quiet and still."

Confused, the kids frowned.

"Okay," someone said. The others nodded, but still the reply was too automatic.

I tilted toward them again. "No," I whispered, "I mean *really* quiet and *really* still. It has to be a solemn oath."

They looked at each other. In my peripheral vision, the thick black slab of reptile hadn't moved in the slightest.

"All right already! We *really* promise!" They were tiring of the redundancy, getting antsy. I shook my head again and lowered my hands in a gesture of slowing down. I reduced my whisper to something like the exhalation of gases from a willow leaf.

"No," I breathed. "I mean *really, really* quiet and *really, really* still."

Now the group gelled in the solidarity of wanting results. They leaned toward me and mimicked me by lowering their hands and whispering, "We *really, really* promise." Remarkably, they intoned this in near-perfect unison. Their voices were delicate, downy feathers floating to the ground. They were ready.

"A friend of mine is going to prove to you just how very safe it is here at night. I want to introduce you to him, but be very calm and accepting. He's shy." I smiled. "Look who is going to sleep over with me tonight." Very, very slowly, like a magician's levitating trick, I raised my hand and pointed to the top of the liner beside the door. The children's eyes matched the speed of my movement. Their heads pivoted owl-like until their eyes were fixed on the snake. No one screamed. No one made a sudden motion. No one appeared to be pondering a desperate escape. That black rat snake had achieved what every teacher dreams of: 100 percent attention from 100 percent of a class. A few faces turned back to me with cockeyed grins. They thought I'd planted a rubber snake.

From my cross-legged position, I flexed the muscles of my legs to levitate myself slowly to a standing position, as if floating upward on a gentle current. I carefully continued at this speed, stalking my way through the children across the floor. When I was standing by the snake, I looked at my wards to make sure all were watching. They were. It was a rare moment. I probably could have handed out Game Boys to each child, and they would have set the electronic gadgets aside unnoticed.

I gently stroked the snake at its thickest part, the scales dry and slightly textured from their centered keels.

Its thick tubular body went into a slow and graceful mode of static locomotion; that is, it moved upon itself without going anywhere, like a slippery knot trying to tighten itself, a reptilian spiral. The mouths of those who had smirked now hung open, and their eyes shone like coins, reflecting the scattered light from the door.

"This is the black rat snake that helps me guard my food supplies. He's a constrictor. He's big enough to eat rats." The snake's movements ceased, then its head lifted, and its dark tongue tested the air. "He smelling me—and you. I want him to stay here with me, so think friendly thoughts."

"Will he bite you?" someone asked.

"Not if I leave him alone."

"If he did, would you die?"

I shook my head. "Rat snakes aren't venomous. They kill by squeezing."

"Could he squeeze you to death?"

I smiled and shook my head. "I'm too big"—and before the inevitable question—"and so are you."

We all sat in the semi-dark of the tipi staring at our guest as in a movie theater. No one said a word. The rat snake settled and displayed its infinite patience by remaining as still as the tipi itself. It probably wondered how the heck it had gotten into this situation: stuck in an enclosure with thirteen humans.

We still had chores to do and supper to cook, so we filed out respectfully, like Cherokee stalking through Catawba territory. As each student passed by the snake, none cringed or spasmed in fear or pulled a face. They studied the creature with interest, some even pausing to get a little closer. A few sniffed it to check for scents. As a group, our deportment was admirable, and each child exited the tipi with a notch of maturity carved into his experience. They had demystified the snake and, in part, the coming night. One slice of the unknown had become known. Snakes were not marauding ambushers; they were actually pretty laid-back.

Throughout supper and campfire time, spirits held high. No one fell prey to depression or homesickness or fear of the dark. But later, a few eyes lingered on me as I retired to my tipi for the night. If I survived the night, perhaps they could accept the possibility of being at home in the wild.

The rat snake loitered exactly where we had left it. I didn't build a fire that night. I thanked the reptile for its lesson and drifted off to sleep, knowing that his work shift was about to begin and happy for this predator to roam all over my living area. The balance of predator and prey was needed inside my tipi just as it was outside.

When I awoke at daybreak, the snake had gone. All my digits remained, and there were no constriction grooves spiraling across my chest to show that it had almost squeezed the life out of me. When the kids emerged from their tents for breakfast, they asked a thousand questions about what it was like to sleep with a snake, and everybody wanted to know where the snake was now.

"I don't know," I said. "That's the thing about wild animals. They're phantoms. They just appear and disappear so effortlessly, so unexpectedly. They have the disappearing act down perfectly."

One little girl intently scanned the woods around my tipi. Then under her breath she said, "I hope he spends the night with me in my tent tonight."

There was so much hope in her eyes that a chill ran up my spine.

~ 16 ~

Copper Kong

But that rat snake hadn't been my camp's first encounter with a serpent. On the land that I had been leasing in the mountains, there had been others, one of which established itself as legend.

Around my tipi, I had built open-air log shelters for the children, and so our little village on the ridge above the Etowah was both primitive and multicultural: a Plains tipi alongside two Iroquois longhouses. Our craft project for the session was to make lacrosse sticks from carved hickory branches heated over fire and then bent to shape. We were looking forward to the work and planned a grand finale game on our last day. As we spread out and searched the forest for properly sized limbs, one camper called from the rock outcrop that overlooked the valley.

"Cop-per-head!"

The announcement came in a tired, familiar, singsong voice that smacked of routine. My campers were becoming veterans in the venomous reptile category. On the occasion of finding our first copperhead on day one, the event had been decidedly more exciting: mouths hanging open, eyes lit up and asking the question: *Are we safe here?*

Whenever we came across a rattlesnake or a copperhead on our jaunts away from base camp, I caught it, gave a brief snake-identification lesson that repeated the last, carried it a safe distance from our location, and released it. The difference this time was that we weren't down near the river. We were standing just a few dozen steps from our sleeping quarters. As I headed toward the rock outcrop, I replayed the hackneyed tone of the finder's declaration. *Maybe*, I thought, *the lackluster timbre of the call was due to a less than positive ID*. I was betting on a corn snake.

When I first saw Copper Kong—the name we eventually bestowed upon him—I felt like Michael Rennie in *The Lost World*, that old science fiction movie in which he stumbled upon an island where dinosaurs still roamed the jungle. Copper Kong was huge, all out of proportion for his species—like Popeye's forearms. Reptile books routinely estimate the maximum length for these snakes at three feet. Copper Kong exceeded four and was as thick at his midsection as a deli loaf of salami. With all the voles in the meadow and rats and mice in the old chicken house on the property, it made sense for a snake this size to thrive up on the ridge.

Normally, I capture a snake right away before it can slither off into a nook or cranny where I can't get at it, but Copper Kong looked strong enough to challenge me to an arm wrestling contest. How had the camper who had made the report edited the awe out of his voice? Glancing at him revealed the answer: I had misread his call. He was beyond awe . . . well into the domain of choked-up terror. It was a wonder he'd found a voice at all.

The rest of the campers gathered around us and stood quietly. It was a strange tableau of stone children encircling a wayward strand of Medusa's hair on steroids.

I am comfortable with snakes, even think them beautiful. At the same time, I respected the pit viper's venom and its instinct to defend itself. I had probably displaced fifty to sixty venomous snakes from various places to safer surroundings, safer both for snakes and for humans. But no snake's strength might have rivaled my own—until this one.

Except during mating, rattlers and copperheads are rather sluggish creatures unless bothered, and in case you're wondering: Yes, catching one definitely falls into the category of bothering it. The more I pictured myself capturing this reptilian giant, the more I reassembled the memory of Johnny Weissmuller, bareback on a fourteen-foot crocodile, spinning round and round underwater, stabbing its back in one of the Tarzan movies. Even as a boy, when I—pushed back into my theater seat as far as I could go—had watched this fight to the death, I knew it was a doll attached to a rubber lizard, all of it set on a rotating spit. The effect might have been hokey, but the scene had imprinted a lasting image. Now I was conjuring the image as a reference on what to do next.

Through the trees I caught a glimpse of our camp and those open-air shelters, which, of course, were open-snake shelters, too. These children were my responsibility. I imagined this snake visiting their shelters at night or checking out mouse-scent inside my tipi or, worse, inside the deep pocket of one of our sleeping bags. "The Snake in the Sleeping Bag," a *Reader's Digest* First Person Award winner, had been one of those unforgettable magazine articles I had saved as a boy. I wasn't sure my sleeping bag could hold both this snake *and* me, but thinking about it made my toes curl.

With practiced caution, I caught the snake behind the head and quickly realized that I had *not* underestimated his strength. When I lifted him and he jerked to free himself, it was as though I had grabbed onto a loose fire hose running a full jet of water. As a rule, I walked a venomous snake to its new home, carrying my passenger in my hands. For Copper Kong, I needed a container of some kind. I didn't want to compete against his muscular writhing for long. Each time he tried to pry his massive head from my grasp, I lost a centimeter of purchase that I had to regain with improvised legerdemain.

My assistant, Tyler, a great kid who would walk through burning quicksand with me, gave me a tentative look—as though I might have taken on a project a little too ambitious this time.

"I'm going to need to put him inside something," I said, keeping my voice steady so as to impart a sense of calm to the group. (Translation: *"Tarzan in heap big water buffalo dung this time."*)

"What about the big plastic bucket we use for bathing?" Tyler suggested. (Translation: *"I would love to run and get it for you. I would love to run anywhere else right now."*)

"There's no top for that bucket." (*I'm thinking more of a Dumpster.*)

Tyler's face went blank. (*Tyler pictured himself carrying the back end of this monster for a mile, remembering the putrid musk that an angry snake squirts from its anus.*)

I paused for a second to think what to do. (*How did that scene with Tarzan and the crocodile end?*)

"Hey!" Tyler said, raising a finger. "My pillowcase!"

A memory popped into my head. Once, when I had done a demonstration on fire-making at a scout jamboree, the speaker before me had been a snake handler. He had kept his snakes in cloth bags tied by drawstrings at the top. That guy was a professional. A pillowcase is a cloth bag. That was it! I nodded to Tyler, and he took off running.

Like an entourage of serpent worshippers following the high priest of snakedom, we walked back to the meadow and awaited Tyler and his pillowcase. The campers formed a wide circle, eager to watch the transfer from hand to bag. They speculated as to the technique I might use to place the snake in the bag. I listened with interest—after all, I had never put a giant snake into a pillowcase.

In headfirst? I imagined putting my hand down into the bag with the snake, and that option was out. What about tail-first? At the moment of release, the snake's head would be above my hand, traveling downward. Maybe if I opted for tail-first and threw the head down to get it into the bag quickly. That could work.

Tyler came charging in like a Pony Express courier, breathing hard, his eyes riveted to Copper Kong, in his hands a reassuringly large pillowcase. As he stared at our captive, I told him my plan. Halfway through, I asked him if he was listening to me. When he looked at me blankly, I started over and explained the plan again. Here it was: Tyler would use his two hands and I my one free hand to form a triangle with the opening of the pillowcase. When I had lowered the snake three-quarters of the way into the bag, I would count to three. On "three," I would throw the snake's head down into the bag and close the bag with both my hands. Also at "three," Tyler would let go to give me full control over the bag so that he could step back out of harm's way. He liked that last part.

Here's what I imagined would happen: I lift the snake high enough to thread its tail into the triangular mouth of the pillowcase. I lower Copper Kong until we are eye to eye. I count to "three" and throw the snake's head downward. The snake disappears into the bag. Tyler releases the bag and steps away. At the speed of a magician's slight of hand, I gather the material at the opening and hold the weighty bag with its sagging tangle of snake, tamed and inert at the bottom, just like the snake handler I had once seen.

Snake in a poke. *No problemo.*

"Ready?" I said.

Tyler pressed his lips into a tight line and nodded.

I let the snake hang from one hand as I took the lip of the bag with the other. I lifted the reptile as high as I could to get its tail into the bag. It felt like a Nautilus exercise. We had to lower the bag as far as I could reach to get him inside. Gripping the triangle we had made of the bag's opening, I looked at Tyler and realized that I had never seen his eyes this close . . . or this big.

"One . . ." I counted.

Tyler swallowed.

"Two . . ."

I swallowed. Time stopped. The wind died. Not a bird was singing anywhere. Tyler and I were in burning quicksand.

"Three!"

Quick as lightning, I threw . . . maybe a little harder than I'd planned. My free hand hurried to cinch the top of the pillowcase. Tyler's fingers were releasing right on schedule. We were in perfect sync—but already it was too late.

It was surreal, a gravity-defying magic trick. There was no snake in the bag. I couldn't accept what I was seeing: Copper Kong was *above* us—suspended in the air, at least two feet above our heads, and on his way down.

It was raining venomous snake.

Out of pure reflex, I pulled back without knowing I was doing it. My body leaned into the acceleration like a sprinter, only backward. Somewhere in my peripheral vision, Tyler, in a mirror image, performed the same lightning-fast retreat. We looked like two bodies taking the full impact of a bomb that had just detonated in a pillowcase between us. The ring of spectators widened like the bomb's shock wave. All eyes held to the reptile falling from the sky.

If I had ruminated for hours over the feasibility of this venture in snake-bagging, I never would have imagined the possibility of the creature springing off its tail to sail above us. Think of the strength needed to soar two feet above my head: I am six feet tall, and the bottom of the bag was probably two feet above the ground. How many times had I read that snakes can strike approximately two-thirds of their body length? But that is likely on a horizontal thrust. Copper Kong had rocketed six feet vertically, reaching an apex of eight feet above the earth!

The sound of that enormous body flopping onto the ground comes back to me as vividly as the image of the flying snake.

Flump!

Imagine hurling a four-foot-long loaf of salami at an adobe wall, and you've got the idea.

Now, let's think again about that concept of "bothering" a snake. I had hung this one by the neck, thrown it into a bag, and watched it spring out and up to drop eight feet back to the earth. Where exactly does that fall on the scale of angering a snake? Judging from Copper Kong's first posturing in the grass . . . very high.

One basic rule of snake-catching is: *The first time you catch any snake is always the easiest time you will catch said snake.* Copper Kong was coiled and defensive and had every reason to be unhappy with me.

After some strategic maneuvering, I caught him again and took a firm double grip, one hand behind his jaws, the other just anterior to the anus. Turning to Tyler, I said, "I'm going to walk him out to the highway."

Tyler frowned. "That's two miles, isn't it?"

I nodded. "Keep everyone together until I get back. Why don't you tell them a story?" (Translation: *If I don't return by supper, pile the kids in the van and get out while you can. There may be more, and this one could be the runt of the litter.*)

"Don't worry. We'll be fine. You take care." (*We'll be locked in the van. If you're not back in an hour, we're outta here.*)

I walked the dirt road to the paved county road and then another mile and a half to the main highway.

All along the walk I concentrated on holding Kong's head with just the right tension, loose enough not to hurt him, firm enough not to endanger me. It's a fine line. For most of our stroll, his head turned back in an awkward quarter-pivot, his mouth agape and his fangs hinged open straining to angle toward me. Yellow-orange venom oozed from those long, curved, hypodermic teeth until my right hand looked as if I had dipped it in a bucket of orange juice.

When I got to the highway, I walked another half-mile before entering the woods and giving Copper Kong a gentle toss into the leaves. He was worn out. So was I. I stood a while watching him, knowing I might never see anything like him again.

As I gazed at his record-breaking bulk, I went back over the afternoon from his point of view: Lazing by the heat of a sunny rock. Vibrations of footsteps from the archenemy human . . . not one, but many. Surrounded. Caught by the tall one. Removed from the security of the earth. Manacled by warm-blooded hands. Abducted. Lynched over a bag. Thrown downward at high speed. For a millisecond, imprisoned and claustrophobic. Quick review of the rare spring-tail maneuver granddaddy had taught in case he was ever dropped into a bag. An all-or-nothing lunge straight up toward the sky. Flying. Stalling. Free-falling. *Oomph!* Ah, earth. But no time to relax. The enemy returns. Coil. Protect. Damn, caught again! Gag, bounce, gag, bounce. Bite, bite, bite. Nothing. Squirt anyway. Gag, bounce. Try to bite again. Bite, bite, bite. Still nothing. Squirt again. And again. Fatigue. Surrender. Dull stupor. How long will it take to manufacture again all that wasted venom? *Flop!* Ow! Ah, earth. Stillness. Whew! More stillness. Is the nightmare over? Gather senses and evaluate. According to internal GPS, it's a full-day's journey due west to get back to big brother. I'll rest up first.

"Sorry," I said, my apology meager but sincere. I turned and jogged back to my campers.

A few years from now, when this story has had ample time to evolve through the telling and retelling of distorted details, it may sound something like this:

I heard of a group of kids in a summer camp who found a nine-footer. Biggest copperhead on record. They say it weighed ninety pounds. The guy in charge had the thing captured—tied up in a sack—when it untied the knot, Houdini-style, coiled itself into a spring, and shot straight up into the air two feet over their heads. The snake dragged the camp leader a couple of miles out to a highway and left him there to be run over by a semi.

No one would ever believe the part about the snake flying two feet above our heads.

~ 17 ~

Crossing the Threshold

On many days I didn't step into my truck, walk on concrete or boards or any other kind of flooring, or hear a human voice. This might be a trilogy of rites, a secret formula for entering into suspended reverence. What an easy recipe. Tipi-life, it became clear, is a time-rich experience filled with spiritual incident. Often the duration of this state stretched into days.

I don't know that anyone ever gets a permanent hold of reverence and fixes it into place alongside the functions of breathing and pumping blood through the body. Some have come close. Keeping a lasting grip on this beatific state is like the quest for moral perfection. We're never going to get there, but we would be much less than who we are if we didn't strive for it. Every time that I achieved a quieter way for longer durations, I was permanently better for it and more equipped to engage the ascent into higher levels of reverence on the occasion of its next visit.

Maybe that's what sent the raccoon to my tipi.

Did my quiet days resonate with the modest utterances of the forest? Does the modern human still emit pheromones through its pores just as our paleo-ancestors did, to disclose our seemingly private moods and personalities to the living things around us? I've read the scientific studies; I've pored over the experiments. It's all compelling and sensible. Yet I don't know how to explain with certainty the interaction between the raccoon and me. I can only tell you what happened.

I took long walks through the forest with my bow. Sometimes I shot many arrows, sometimes only a few. I wasn't a hunter. I had given that up long ago when I discovered that at the center of me lay a craving—perhaps an evolved need—to pursue some other bond with wild animals, one that didn't involve death. Because I considered archery my art, I shot arrows at rotten stumps, shadows, and bright leaves on the ground. This is the game that T. H. White's young Arthur called "Rovers" in *The Once and Future King*, and the term instantly became an addition to my vocabulary.

The deer eventually realized that the land around the strange smoking cone was a place of refuge. Amid the sporadic thunder of the hunting season's gunfire, Medicine Bow became an island of safe harbor. The deer saw me daily just as I saw them. In time, they knew not to run from me in panic. They simply trotted away. They would never surrender their wildness, of course, as long as I didn't cross that line of responsibility toward wildness by offering food. Which I never did. Nor did they lose their rightful legacy of wariness. It was as it should have been.

In my wanderings I discovered the remnants of pioneer homes, ancient trails, and other streams waiting for me across the watershed. I moved quietly and observed. And was observed. I spiraled through this new land to understand how each part of it fit with the rest and how I fit within it all.

"Stay wild," I often said to any animal I encountered. *Hello and farewell,* it translated. *Live the best life possible.*

As the wild creatures dissolved into the shadows with this blessing, did the phrase take on some familiarity for them?

On my way home after roving at dusk of a winter's day, a sound above in a giant sourwood—whose trunk was contorted like a snapshot of a whiplash—stopped me. Thirty feet up a raccoon clung to the sourwood's bark, his bushy ringed tail disappearing around the back of the tree.

Elly was scouting the way ahead somewhere, so I stopped and waited. How long could the raccoon's curiosity hold out? In a matter of seconds, he peeked out from around the trunk and studied me with curious eyes. His appraisal seemed unmarked by the impetuosity of youth. His inspection had a stateliness to it, and he appeared a little grizzled and gray. He was an elder. As we stared at one another, I wondered what I looked like to him.

Here's a two-legged carrying the long, curved stick that I know to fear. Feathers protrude at an angle from one shoulder—the flying death sticks! Yet he stands relaxed. This man is in no hurry. I do not smell the talon-sharp scent of danger emanating from his body—but there is the dreaded dog up ahead. No dog can be trusted!

I spoke to my masked neighbor much the way I would whisper to an introverted child with troubled eyes, just a friendly greeting. Old Raccoon kept looking at me. I had seen piercing eyes like this all my life. *What is it you intend to do?* his eyes said.

I spoke again, telling him that he could be at ease with me if he felt he could find that kind of trust, but that he was smart to be so wary. We humans do not have a good track record with the wild things. He kept staring.

"Stay wild, Old Raccoon," I said and continued on my way home.

I imagined his relief. Through his eyes I could see myself leaving his territory, my silhouette diminishing in the distance. Through his ears I heard my footsteps fading in the leaves. Old Raccoon's world of quiet gathered back around him. Up ahead lay a similar place for me: the tipi. Our worlds were alike. In fact, they were the same.

Two nights later the temperature dropped into the teens. After stockpiling wood and bathing, I stoked the fire and read by candlelight—twice having to secure the door flap against the wind. I extended the liner across the doorway and pinned it to the ground with a milk crate at either side.

Several hours after I had blown out the candle, more flapping at the door woke me. Then a rustling sound came from the liner. In the light of the fire, one of the milk carts moved from a bulge in the canvas. I sat up for a better look, trying to decide if my sleepy eyes were playing a trick on me. The wind had let up a bit. I couldn't understand the movement at the door. Had Elly finally tired of braving the cold?

Old Raccoon slipped through the folds of canvas past the milk crates and walked toward me. I didn't move. Keeping the fire pit between us, he stopped behind my reflector-stone, his eyes sparkling with flecks of yellow from the flames. He tottered to one side briefly, as if the Earth had unexpectedly tilted by a few degrees.

Distemper, parvovirus, and rabies immediately came to mind. This kind of unusual behavior in a wild animal often indicates one of these diseases. Humans should avoid contact with animals displaying such symptoms. In fact, I had once encountered a different raccoon that suffered from parvo. Its eyes had buzzed with a nervous tension that made me wonder if wild creatures could fall prey to insanity.

Tonight was different, though. Old Raccoon's eyes looked focused and serene. Our mutual inspection of one another suggested an alliance of acceptance. Never had I seen the eyes of a wild creature so filled with a single profound question. But what that question was, I didn't know.

I got out of bed, took down my towel from the drying line, folded it once as a kind of protective glove, and knelt beside Old Raccoon. As I eased the towel over him like a blanket, he didn't even turn his head, remaining focused on the fire. All his strength went into the maintenance of his equilibrium, as though the journey to my home had taken his all.

That this wild animal had entered my lodge when I was in it surprised me enough; that he approached a fire and stood before it was uncanny. Was it an act of desperation against the cold? I slipped my bare fingers into the chilled fur under his belly and chest, and lifted him. He showed no sign of protest.

I carried him around the fire pit and gently laid him on his side before the halo of warmth radiating off the reflector-stone. Seemingly resigned to his new surroundings, he closed his eyes.

I stroked his head for a while and tucked the ends of the towel over the pads of his feet so they wouldn't overheat. When I spoke to him, he opened his eyes briefly, but soon he seemed beyond hearing me, so I remained silent as I lightly stroked the fur along his ribs, keeping a gentle, steady rhythm of reassurance.

After a time, I slipped back into my own bedding and lay on my side watching his ribs rise and fall in tiny increments. I whispered a prayer and tucked my forearm lightly behind his spine so he would feel my presence. For a long time I watched him, until finally my eyes closed, and I joined him in sleep.

In the morning Old Raccoon was dead. I buried him in the towel and spoke words for the journey of his spirit. Elly looked on with unusual acceptance, the sanctity of death somehow overriding all her instincts of predator-prey relationships. When I had finished tamping the cold earth over his grave, I looked up the valley at my tipi and tried to imagine his intent the night before. What must it have taken for him to cross that barrier of canvas? Had illness robbed him of instinct? Had desperation forced upon him a desperate act? Or could it have been something else entirely?

Had pheromones wafted between us that day as he studied me from the sourwood? Had my intentions floated to him through those communicative molecules of scent that scientists tell us we humans still exude but have lost a conscious capacity to interpret? Did he recognize in me an ally? Was this, in fact, the same raccoon?

Teresa had a book on animal rehabilitation, and the next time I visited her, I planned to see what I could learn about Old Raccoon's symptoms. Whatever the answers, though, I walked especially quietly that day and thought constantly of the strange visitation. It had been an honor, a privilege in some arcane way, and my mind insisted on dissecting the event for more understanding.

But what can you do with such limited information? You guess. Teresa's book didn't provide a definitive answer about Old Raccoon's condition. Eventually I decided that I should think less about analyzing the event and simply accept it. Mystery does, after all, have its place in our lives. Releasing the incident from introspection also seemed the respectful thing to do for Old Raccoon's sake.

Temporarily towel-less, I built a fire next to the creek that night. I bathed and dried and blew on my fingers against the bitter cold. There by the water, my fingers painfully, numbly rebellious in the workings of buttons and snaps reminded me of the time hypothermia had seized me, when much younger, on the Chattooga River. On that occasion I would have crawled over her cubs into a she-bear's lap to get warm.

A human is probably more terrifying to a raccoon than a bear is to a hapless, shivering canoeist. I had been lucky in my youthful folly: A kind man had miraculously appeared in that remote place and saved my life.

I wished I could have done as well for Old Raccoon.

~ 18 ~

Harvest

Two of my favorite experiences *for* Medicine Bow were hearing excited school kids arrive for a class and then listening to their quieter voices fade down the trail when their time here was done. Hearing the forest silence suddenly flooded with the sounds of children—and vice versa—gave me the perspective of listening through the forest's ears.

On their morning arrivals I might be reading or working on a craft project before my fire when their conversations bubbled up from the direction of the meadow. They were full of the primordial joy and anticipation of adventure. A school day in the woods! They didn't realize they were carrying their city voices like slashing machetes.

I always smiled when I heard them. I looked forward to their visits, too. When they walked back to their bus at the end of our time together, they always carried with them a piece of the natural serenity that resided here as a part of the flow of life. If I did my job well, more than the volume of their voices would change.

What a gift of a workplace—a forest. Unless I visited a school, my workday started and ended in the woods. My duties unfolded among hickories and hemlocks, woodpeckers and crows. All ages of students came, from third graders to octogenarians. We worked with wood and fire, river cane and the leaves and bark of medicinal plants.

All my qualifications came from the time I had spent in a forest—beginning with the days when I was no older than my youngest grammar school students. They don't frame those kinds of diplomas. Even if they did, there wasn't a wall on which to hang one. I smile when I think back to my college days. I changed majors every year and a half trying to figure out what I was going to be. And all the time . . . I already *was*.

To this day I still shake my head at the wonder of my job description and never take the blessing for granted.

But I often think back to the phone call I'd made to cancel my spot at the medical school that had accepted me after college. The act was as clear as swimming to the surface of deep water to feel the sun on my face, to breathe again, to see the details of the world around me as if all things had just been created fresh and new and settled into their perfect places.

The children soon defected to the dignity of the natural world around them. Confronted with the peacefulness of the tipi, the patience of the trees, and the tantalizing possibility of encountering wildlife, they softened their voices. Won over by the overwhelming grandeur and sensible reserve of the forest, they followed me into the lesson I had planned for them.

One day, I stopped the group in the dark, cathedral space beneath tall, interlacing hemlocks. "You are standing in *the real world*," I said. They looked around. "The real world," I continued, "was here before us and will be after us. There was a time when all people in every corner of the world found their every need in the forest, field, river, and ocean. Or desert, jungle, or tundra. There were no stores, you know . . . not a single one."

Letting that sink in, I looked up into the boughs of the evergreens and counted all the bounteous gifts that *Tsuga canadensis* afforded the Cherokee: three different foods, a pink dye, wood that has "swallowed fire," human scent absorber, hide-tanning chemical, cordage, and thread-sized kindling.

"If that time should come again," I said, "if all the stores closed, people will discover that the forest still has everything that we need."

"I've heard my uncle use those words, 'the real world,'" one child said, puzzled, looking around at the thick trunks and lofty carpet of needles, the crease lines on her forehead deepening. "I don't think he was talking about this, though."

"People have moved so far away from these direct provisions," I said, "that they forget which portion of the planet is *the real world*."

She looked lost, so I tried again.

"The grocery store seems real, doesn't it? When you're hungry, it's a magical place of instant solutions. You can get most anything you want there. But what if trucks stopped delivering all that food to the stores?"

"Why would they do that?" someone asked.

I shrugged. "We run out of gas?"

"How could we run out of gas?" they asked.

"Well, do you know where gasoline comes from?"

They jumped on that one: "Gas stations!"

"But gasoline is trucked to the gas stations." I smiled. "It comes from someplace else."

This is how conversations progress. We work our way from the children's familiar world back to the accumulation of fossil fuel material over eons.

"Hey, do you want to see a grocery store that never closes, no matter what?" I asked.

I considered the hemlocks for a moment, but these children wouldn't enjoy the taste of its inner bark. It wouldn't matter that I could spout off a list of ten essential nutrients contained in the bark, including the survivalist's top two culinary treasures—protein and fat. Nutrients don't mean much to a ten-year-old. Taste does.

We walked down to the creek to the big persimmon tree that had begun to drop its fruit—just in time to see one plop into the water. I took off my boots and waded out. Everyone sampled the delicious pulp. There's nothing like a natural sweet treat to kick-start some youthful enthusiasm about the woods.

"This is a female tree," I said, as these once tentative foragers sucked their fingers clean. "It hands out fruit yearly. It works completely independent of us. It's going to make fruit whether we stop here or not. It's a free grocery store. This aisle is open only for a couple of months out of the year, but other aisles open up elsewhere all the time."

"Wait," a thoughtful girl interrupted. "There are girl trees and boy trees?"

And so it goes.

Whenever I hosted new students—especially grammar school kids—our initial conversation went pretty much the same, after the introductions:

"You smell like smoke."

I nodded. "So will you when you leave here."

"You really live out here?" another said, pointing to the tipi, "In that?"

I nodded again.

"Cool!" a boy said. All eyes remained on the tipi. Then as if the idea dropped onto his head like Newton's apple, he quickly turned back to me, his eyes electric with hope. "Can we go in?"

"Sure, if—"

But it was always too late. A stampede poured downhill from the group campsite toward the tipi, and I had to whistle to regain control. But the stentorian command delivered by their classroom teacher drowned my shrill, through-the-teeth whistle. They froze like inmates caught in a spotlight during a prison break. It wasn't the first time these kids had heard this tone in her voice. She could have done no better by firing a cannon.

The students stared at their teacher as if that cannon were filled with canister and grapeshot and trained directly on every one of them. I gave the teacher a little signal with my hand, assuring her that lighting the powder wouldn't be necessary.

"Let me tell you a little bit about how to move around in a tipi," I said. "It's different from your home."

The children listened. But my speech always seemed to be an unnecessary preparation—"pre-dundant," you might call it. Once they stepped inside, the tipi had a way of teaching the same lesson without words. Respectfully quiet, they looked around with eyes that soaked up everything. If they talked, they whispered. Just like an empty cathedral, the tipi's interior space demanded it.

Settled in the lodge, we sat in a circle, and they asked a hundred questions about the accoutrements of my home.

"What's this for?"

"That's my urinal."

"What's a 'your-null'?"

"I pee in that at night. My bathroom gets pretty cold outside."

"You pee in a mayonnaise jar?"

"Well, I don't use it for mayonnaise anymore."

Some of the children giggled, while others were quiet, reconsidering me.

"Do you really live here? You don't go home at night?"

"Yes to both questions. This *is* my home."

"Do you have a wife?"

"I have a female friend. Her name is Teresa. She's not really a tipi person. She visits sometimes."

"What do you eat . . . nuts and bark and stuff? Do you hunt bears?"

"This morning I had oatmeal and nuts. The bears and I leave each other alone."

"Where do you get oatmeal?"

"At a grocery store in town." They looked confused, the troops drifting into what I believed to be disappointment. "But I got the nuts from the hickory trees." I waited to see if I had redeemed myself from the store-bought oats. They had no idea of the dedication it takes to pick enough nutmeat out of hickory shells for a meal. Much more challenging than hunting bears.

"*You* go to a *store?*"

"Sure."

I had broken the rules for living in the woods, it seemed. They wanted me to eat raw snakes, run down deer, and battle wild boars, tooth-to-tooth, to the death. They continued to stare in disbelief.

Then I realized that I had misread the question screwing up in their faces. It wasn't disappointment; it was some kind of awe.

Finally someone said something I wouldn't have guessed in a thousand tries. "You mean . . . regular people get to see you?"

I had to run the words through my head again before I got it. *Tarzan Goes to New York.* I laughed, but no one else did. The smile slowly relaxed from my face as I realized that they were dead serious. Now they saw that there were more choices about how to live than they had imagined.

Dear God, I thought. *I have their attention. Help me light a fire in them today!*

When you live in a tipi, it's not the same world you see when the average person steps from his house to assess the weather. Turn the knob, crack the door, stick your head outside, and look at the sky. "Let's see what this day is like."

Living in a tipi, you already know. You never left. You never forget the weather. You don't dress for a dash from back door to car. You dress for *the real world.*

The trees are not background scenery, not three-dimensional fixtures defining the open spaces and obstructions of the forest. Trees are alive, doing what you do in their own way: making a living, dealing with the elements. Their living tissues sometimes can provide food or medicine. Their discarded parts can provide other treasures: firewood, fire-making wood, craft material, cordage, tinder, or insulation.

Trees and other plants take on a metaphysical presence. Their patience and endurance become evident. When you touch the skin of a tree, you feel admiration. A tree's functions—all the textbook terms that you once filed away for a high school science test—now transcend the wood-pulp pages of academics and take their places in the immediacy of life, in the formula that explains the very possibility of life for every creature.

It is perhaps the most profound of prayers to remember that trees are the primary agents for capturing the sun's energy for use in these mountains. It's the energy that fuels everything—running with deer, lifting a massive stone, and turning a page in this book. Each act begins with the sun.

But using this energy hinges upon something capturing it for us. Trees do that. This fact should remain in the forefront of our minds every day, just as subterranean crude oil should reside in our consciousness as we drive our cars and keep an eye on the gas gauge. But does it? Perhaps we lost the reason to remember because we have evolved from that "primitive" state of living that connected us directly to our resources.

When you live in a tipi, you know things that you wouldn't otherwise know. You live connected to *the real world*. If, as you read this book, you're inside a building— which way is the wind blowing? Chances are that you won't know. In a tipi, you know because you have set the direction of your smoke flaps downwind to draw the smoke as efficiently as possible. If the wind has shifted, smoke backing into the tipi gives you an immediate weather update. You have to act. You are connected.

What is the phase of the moon? When you step from your tipi at night, the moon is your mistress. She pulls your eye with her beauty, and you take note of her whims. When did she arrive? The time of her rising is different every day by almost an hour. It continues to surprise me how many adults don't know that fact. A crossword puzzle I recently worked gave the clue "twilight." The eight-letter answer turned out to be "moonrise." This mistake was made by a clever wordsmith, and how many editors did it slip past? What happened to this most basic knowledge of the working of the world?

How can you describe the moon tonight? Waxing? Waning? First quarter? Third quarter? Crescent? Gibbous? Half? New? Is it rising or falling at that particular point in the sky? Can you read the time by it, as with the sun? Which way does the crescent moon point? When you live in a tipi, you know these things. They insinuate into your consciousness. They participate.

If, for example, I want to undertake a day journey by foot and I'm not sure I can return before dark, I plan this trip for the end of the first quarter moon; because as it gets dark, the moon is at its apex, lighting my way, extending twilight, so to speak, for a good four hours. This half-moon lights my way as it slides to the west.

Are there flying squirrels out there? Oh, yes. They make sharp kissing sounds in the night. If you're fast, you can catch them with your flashlight up in the branches and illuminate a white-bellied, spotlighted flight. When I became more aware of these rodents and began to read about flying squirrels, I discovered that they're the most populous mammal in Georgia. Before living in the tipi, I had seen only three in the wild. During tipi-life, they became nightly sightings.

Give a child the project of catching one of these sailing creatures in the beam of his flashlight, and you've handed him the key to a treasure chest. It wells up from the atavistic urge to hunt—something almost all people at some time feel bursting out of them. There's nothing wrong with it. Hunting was once a survival necessity. It might become that again one day. Maybe it's *why* and *how* most modern hunters go about the hunt that turns so many others off.

If we allow children time to live as part of the forest instead of as a visitor, when they get older they might have second thoughts about the "mindless-killing" part of sport-hunting. When I teach young students how to stalk, they tap into a natural desire to be stealthy. It's older than history. But rather than kill, we simply crave sightings of wild animals. We observe. We accrue these memories with the joy of earning and owning the experience—not meat and hide. But there is value in knowing that we could access these resources if the need arose.

The tipi played its part in my students' acceptance of the bloodless hunt. They saw me living among these creatures, with whom I shared a wild space. They heard me speak of these animals as acquaintances. Some animals had earned pet names due to their frequent visits, distinguishing habits, and interactions with me. When a name like "Ragged Ear Squirrel" became fixed in the common vocabulary of our outside life, a new intimacy was born. A previously anonymous squirrel—redundant among the hordes of squirrels seen throughout the children's lives—became a personality. A squirrel, like Ragged Ear, had taken a quantum leap from a meaningless sight witnessed through window glass to a living part of the world, a squirrel, much like each of us, with missions and moods, anticipations and anxieties.

In their tents, the children set down roots at the fringe of tipi-life. They began to probe the real world. Part of the light shed for them in this venture might very well be the lantern-like glow of the tipi at night, a second moon, always in a dependable phase.

One of my nightly rituals was to step away from the tipi to see the canvas of my home luminesce and flicker like a breathing and metabolizing creature. It seemed so much alive that I sometimes felt that I lived inside the belly of a benevolent and edifying beast.

Where is the deepest part of the creek closest to you? Where do the deer sleep? What kind of firewood lasts the night? What is that sound out in the dark that makes you think of a rope twirling and whistling? When you live in a tipi—or maybe like the children, in its shadow—these things are revealed by spoonfuls and avalanches.

The wind is yours. The sky is yours. The night enfolds. At dawn, you step out through the door flap. The day is vibrant, and one of its vibrating components is you.

The tipi was always the hub of the campground. It appeared to emerge from the earth. It had roots. The children's tents surrounded it like tender shoots that had popped up from the parent plant's rhizomes. This network of roots flourished as a growing village. The tipi gave authenticity to the camp.

The children awaken and glean all of this on some level. Maybe they can't articulate it, but they absorb much of it into their sponge-like minds. They are pliable enough to embrace whatever the forest presents to them.

How many times I have aborted a planned activity at the toll of the ringing question, *Hey, what's this?* A child has discovered something new: an egg case of a praying mantis, an oak gall, a blue-tailed skink, a chaotic squadron of crane flies bobbing up and down in a moist cavity in the earth.

Sometimes I purposely carry no lesson plan and wait for the children to show it to me, as a gift, like a fruit that knows exactly when to fall from the tree.

~ 19 ~

A Sense of Touch

In June of that second year in the tipi came my most unforgettable housewarming gift. One morning I left the summer campers, my assistant, and Elly at the fire while I retrieved bark fibers left to soak overnight in the creek. Ahead of me in the grove of laurel that covered the north slope, something moved. My body froze for several minutes as my mind played back the vague details of the motion that my eye had witnessed peripherally.

Something very large—undoubtedly a deer—had run from the laurel thicket past the tipi, yet, after that, something else had moved in the laurel again. I waited. Soon the second creature stirred again. I couldn't make out what it was, but its demeanor was anything but stealthy. In fact, it seemed careless, awkward. I stalked closer.

Within twenty yards, my heart squeezed into a fist, and a soft breath of awe and gratitude released from my chest. A fledgling fawn was wobbling from shrub to shrub, sniffing at the leaves, discovering the world. The spots on its coat shone pristinely white against a perfect golden brown pelage. Every hair glistened, impossibly clean and new. Its stilt-legs appeared as brittle as twigs.

I descended to all fours and continued to creep forward, my eyes riveted to the fawn. The young creature's artless manner of inspecting every stone and twig and patch of moss meant that this was doubtless one of its first probes into the details of its new world. This newborn was a portrait of innocence—a blank slate of consciousness absorbing, smelling, hearing, touching, embarking, operating wholly on curiosity and genetic instinct.

Within ten yards, it became clear she was female. When she finally took notice of me, she stood stock-still and tried to focus her eyes. She showed no fear. I was merely the next novelty of her environment to be investigated. She made a high-pitched bleat and staggered toward me, seemingly without a care in the world. I mimicked the sound—relatively easy to replicate—back to her. She bleated again and approached me in such a natural way that I felt a complete sense of acceptance.

Did she think I was Mama Doe?

In that precious moment, it didn't matter what bad things I had done in my life. All my regrets and transgressions washed away. To stare into those big Coca-Cola-colored eyes, to feel such complete innocence so close felt no different than if an angel had descended on a shaft of downy white light to bless me for the morning.

She put her cool, wet nose in my face. The wetness and the warm breath that poured over my woodsmoke-scented cheek came like a baptism. She half-circled me and approached again, sidling up next to me, hips to hips, ribs to ribs. Her little wet nose probed around my armpit area, inserted itself into my T-shirt sleeve, pushed against my triceps, and she began sucking at my skin.

She was trying to nurse.

For a full minute, I watched her as she tried in vain to suckle from my arm, craning my head around to watch a once-in-a-lifetime experience, smiling not unlike a proud mother as this fawn searched for milk up my sleeve.

Common sense told me not to leave my scent on her, but all forest wisdom and pragmatism surrendered to connect with the moment. When she stopped sucking, I raised my hand and reached back to touch her. As my hand poised over her, I reconsidered the ethics of what I was about to do.

Don't touch her, I thought. You know better.

Then the rationalizations poured in. Because I handled so much wood, my hands stayed very dry in tipi-life—virtually without oil and probably scentless. Plus, I had been crawling in the dirt. I was practically Earth personified. As she nuzzled me in the search for a nipple, I knew I would probably never have this chance again. I *needed* to touch her, to glide my hand across that perfect coat.

Very lightly I stroked the warmth of her body. Her coat was silky. The smooth series of bumps made by her ribs felt much like my own. I stroked once more, from her heart all the way back to the soft flank beside her belly, then I lowered my glowing hand back to the ground.

When my new friend finally accepted that I could supply no nourishment, she backed away a few steps and bleated a complaint. For her sake, it was time to end the encounter. I stood up quickly and walked away. The fawn was stunned, I suppose, that I could move so well on my hind legs. Thankfully she didn't follow.

I made a wide half-circle, stalked back into the grove of mountain laurel, got comfortable, and waited. The fawn remained in place, looking around, unsure what to do. The kids down at the campground let out a cheer from a game they were playing. The fawn turned her head in their direction and stared. The world was full of mysteries.

Moments after the fawn heard the children, though, something in her hereditary wiring closed a circuit on cue. The little doe froze like a lawn statue.

In twenty minutes, the mother returned for her baby, the reunion businesslike and swift. Neither vocalized, but a palpable tension telegraphed through the mother's decisive movements. She seemed to gather up her infant with invisible threads that pulled from her body. Together they ran up the mountain north of my tipi. I listened to them until the voices of my summer campers drowned out the shuffle of hooves in leaves high on the ridge. In my mind, I was with mother and fawn, climbing to the ridge, hearing the invasive sounds of humans down in the valley, feeling the relief of successful escape, driving deeper into the heart of the real world.

That day provided the perfect counterbalance to the night that Old Raccoon had visited me—an event not to be measured or analyzed but absorbed into the whole of life and worn as a lasting patch on a coat of many colors. As with the fox and the vole, we should celebrate the balance rather than the outcome.

~ 20 ~

More Scratches at the Door

Oral tradition tells us that the Native Americans living in the bosom of nature supremely respected the wild things. This regard for life carried over into their social lives as well, and they treated one another with a dignity mindful of individual rights. In a cultural setting centered around a tight tribal bond, they still held personal space in great esteem.

Certainly they were not a perfect people. No culture ever was or is. People are, after all, people. Even after Europeans settled the Americas, there were Native Americans who were selfish, cruel, officious, or dishonest. But the more you study their philosophies the more it becomes clear that their general deportment as human beings has much to teach us, especially in the area of reverence.

Their acknowledgment of the Great Mystery— of a Creator and the gifts of stone, water, wood, leaf, root, creature, and fire—came not in gratitude reserved for a single weekly day of worship. It was a philosophy of mindfulness woven uninterrupted like a living thread through time.

To announce her presence at a friend's tipi, a visitor scratched her fingers across the skin draped over the doorway. It was unthinkable to cross that threshold unasked.

Not so with animals.

Throughout my two winters in a tipi, I awoke many times to find curious and intrepid night callers standing just inside my lodge. Mice are a part of tipi-life. That should come as no surprise. They are so numerous in the forest that they are bound to explore any dry abode that stays in one place long enough to allow an exploratory visit.

Other curious friends, in addition to those we've already seen, included a garter snake, a bat, a box turtle, a wren, a phoebe, various lizards, salamanders, chipmunks, a mole, lots of toads, uncountable spiders and insects, and on one bizarre occasion, a bluetick hound who soundly refused to surrender my bed. But the most daring visitor I hosted in my tipi years was unquestionably the spotted skunk.

Everybody knows the *striped* skunk, which waddles around anywhere it pleases with the bold caveat that it is not to be trifled with—or else! Its spray can cause serious problems if it hits you in the face at close range, not to mention days of malodorous discontent for the recipient. These skunks are most often seen on roads—either walking through a headlight beam at night or as a smear of roadkill that retains even in death the power to alter your car's ambience.

Even cruising along a highway at sixty miles an hour, a traveler can experience the tenacity of the fetid "polecat perfume" that lingers inside the vehicle miles after passing a black-and-white striped corpse. Imagine garlic and mustard mixed together in a nuclear meltdown. It's quite an odor, like an olfactory blow to the solar plexus.

Don't get me wrong. Skunks are not professional assassins of aroma let loose on the world. They really don't want to spray. Once during a summer survival trip at the base of Blood Mountain, I lay in my shelter at twilight and was thoroughly entertained, without incident, by a striped skunk that came inside to investigate. Another time in the middle of the night, while running my summer camp in the national forest, a skunk and I had a minor disagreement over the food supplies that I was guarding. The little night bandit did front handstands several times, pointing the business end of his elevated body at me . . . but never firing.

But there is another skunk in north Georgia, a sleek, athletic one that bears little resemblance to its chunky cousin. The spotted skunk is an energetic and more fun-loving creature. Both are weasels, to be sure, but only the spotted skunk seems to be aware of that classification. He is elongated, shaped the way we expect weasels to look, and stealthy. If you could see the two kinds of skunk moving side by side across open ground, about the only feature that would make you think they might be related is their color-coordinated outfits. They wear different patterns, but the colors are the same.

The first time this particular spotted skunk glanced into view, it was dusk, and it bounded like an undulating shadow, disappearing phantom-like into a hole in a stump just fifteen paces from my tipi. It happened so quickly, I wasn't at all certain what I had seen. I walked over to the burrow. It was too dark for tracks, so I leaned down and sniffed. Nothing.

I didn't mention it to the sixth graders who were camping that night because just-before-bed is not the time to introduce any element of the unknown. Its gait and its long, lithe, and agile silhouette identified it as a weasel of some kind, but it had been too far away and too dark to identify.

The next afternoon, after the kids had left, I was tidying the campground. The community trash can hung ten feet off the ground, suspended by a rope that spanned two trees. Since I was driving to a high school to do programs the following day, I left the garbage hanging, planning to haul it out and drop it in the school's Dumpster.

As the day began to fade, Elly and I sat outside the tipi with one collective eye on the grainy disintegration of twilight and the other on the weasel's stump hole. Soon my thoughts ran toward the next day's classes. Elly stretched out, and I stroked her head until darkness fell. Another day in paradise, but no weasel.

The next morning I untied the trash bin and lowered it to the ground to deposit my breakfast refuse. This bin was the hard plastic type, a flange around the lip to accommodate hinged metal clamps that locked down the lid. Besides this security measure, I had run a rope from one side-handle to the other, lashing the lid to the bin as tightly as possible. It was a veritable garbage vault.

But when I opened it, there smiling up at me—like Br'er Fox caught in the chicken coop—sat the spotted skunk.

"Well," I laughed, "good morning, and how did you manage to do this?"

The skunk seemed completely at ease. I lowered the container gently on its side, and my guest sprang lightly across the open ground to the hole in the stump, vanishing again with an effortless bound. Elly's ears popped up as she raised her head. She looked at the stump, then at me, an urgent question writ upon her face: *What the heck was that, and why aren't we barking up a storm right now?*

When I returned home that late afternoon, my trash bin lashing techniques took on a new complexity— something akin to Egyptian mummy wrapping. Still, on two different mornings within the week, my content little guest was waiting for me in the trash can. I named him Houdi, after Houdini . . . but not completely because he could never seem to get the last part down: the escape.

Unless, perhaps, I was the key to that part of his plan. Which, I suppose, I was.

As fun as it was to see him and set him free, he was learning to depend on human scraps. If he moved on to the next human habitation down the way, he might be killed by dogs or shot by a man who might be overzealous about protecting his precious garbage. So my trash bin lashing skills continued to escalate. Master garbage-guardage became my new quest. At last, with my trash bin impregnable, it was time for Houdi to return to hunting in the wild.

Two nights later, a rustling at my door awoke me. In the dim glow of the coals, Houdi pushed through the canvas, bounded happily across the floor of the tipi, and darted under my official Ambassador to India bed.

Okay, I thought, *there's a skunk underneath my bed. Now what?*

Propped up on one elbow, listening, thinking, I weighed the merits of acceptance against the potential for odoriferous calamity. After a few minutes of deliberating, I got up and lifted the edge of the rock-propped plywood on which I slept—hinging it upward like an old storm cellar door.

Houdi looked up at me with apologetic eyes.

"You don't spray in your sleep, do you?" I asked.

After a frozen second of what had to be a musteline moment of exposed embarrassment, Houdi hopped across the floor and exited my home without issue. He never came back into the tipi, but he did manage to gain entry to the garbage a few more times, forcing me to fanatical levels of garbage security—a career I could seriously consider as a backup if teaching ever fails.

Every chapter of tipi-life has a lesson. What had brought Houdi here? It was almost a repeat performance of Old Raccoon's visit that winter night, but this one with a happier ending. What if I hadn't questioned Houdi about staying the night? Would it have heralded the beginning of an animal bond that most of us secretly covet with the wild? Did I blow my one chance to have a wild ally as Tarzan had?

Or might I have fallen prey to bad judgment? Might I have enjoyed a one-night stand of harmonious cohabitation that, in the second night, would have gone up in fumes? I'll never know. Nobody gets through life without regrets, and Houdi will have to be one of mine.

After the few more successful entries he made into the garbage can . . . and after I *finally* achieved full mastery of garbage security techniques, I never saw him again.

·Which is as it should be.

~ 21 ~

Murder and Redemption

A cocoon of warmth surrounded me as the coals sizzled and I waited for sleep in early spring. The stillness inside my tipi perfectly symbolized my life at that point. I was a long way from anyone: No cars could be heard, no airplanes. It was the kind of quiet that whispers of completeness. Everything I needed lay within the round boundary of my ancient shelter. So contented, I let my body sink into the depths of perfect sleep.

That was when I heard the scream.

My eyes opened and blindly tightened as my ears focused on some distant, unseen place in the night.

As remote as I was in the north Georgia mountains, it made no sense to hear a nine-year-old girl being strangled. But that was what I heard. There was no other scenario that could account for the timbre and volume and pitch of this pitiful cry. My mind composed the picture of a young innocent screaming through her throttled throat as some brutish monster crushed her windpipe with his bare hands. The sound came again and hit me like ice water flung on my chest. Swiftly, I got up, dressed, and thrust my flashlight into my coat pocket.

It couldn't be a nine-year-old girl—at least I hoped it wasn't. It had to be an animal. But which one? I hadn't a clue. I couldn't even narrow it down to size or taxonomical family. This was absurd. I was a working naturalist, and I had no idea what I was hearing out in the night. But I was going to find out.

An unknown animal cry in the backyard is every nature lover's personal invitation to adventure. I *had* to know what could make such a scream. So I stalked through the total blackness of a moonless night toward the eerie, intermittent screams. Feeling my way with my feet and moving in the ultra-slow-motion fundamental to stalking, I made very little progress in the first minutes. The complete darkness impeded me not because of objects in my path but because my sense of balance was being tested in ways I had not experienced. You don't realize how much you depend on eyesight for physical orientation until you try balancing on one leg in a darkness so complete that you cannot see your hand in front of your face. I wavered . . . often, spending long periods with both feet on the ground, reestablishing my sense of balance.

The screams continued. Determined, I inched on, wanting to get close enough to switch on my flashlight and spot the animal. Then, another gem of animal lore tucked away in my treasure chest for teaching, I would go back to bed.

It wasn't to be.

In absolute darkness, my sense of balance so thoroughly failed me that, while supporting myself on one leg and probing for my next step, I fell over on my side. Amazingly, I hadn't known that I was falling *until* I hit the ground. As far as I could tell in that startled moment, a moving wall of earth had crested like a wave and blindsided me. So much for the little cilia in my semicircular canals.

I lay on the ground for a while assessing my body parts and wondering if I could glue together my pride. The animal—whatever it was—ran off, galloping through the leaves, no doubt sniggering at the stalker who literally had fallen from grace.

Had I learned anything? Yes, that in total darkness I could stalk about as well as a manatee on a pogo stick. Before you laugh, though, try this: put down this book, stand up, balance on one leg for ten seconds, then close your eyes tightly.

Seriously, try it.

Almost immediately you'll experience a queasy alarm in your gut that announces you have lost some control. We use our eyes and their sense of horizon far more than we might think. Balance on one leg again, but this time look straight up so the horizon isn't visible peripherally. Same results.

But night balance can be improved, I discovered. I worked at it. I stalked more at night. Inside the tipi, I practiced balancing on one leg and closing my eyes. Blind people learn to compensate. There's no reason that the rest of us can't, too.

It took five years for this strangled-girl riddle—and the practice of stalking with eyes closed—to reach its satisfactory denouement. When that next chilling invitation to a child's strangulation came, I was prepared. Again it was a moonless, spring night, dark as pitch (which might be a condition favorable for this scenario). After a laborious stalk, with no more than five or six yards left between me and the mystery screamer, the gruesome sound continued piercing the night. Even so close, the sound was still startling and otherworldly.

The click and beam of my flashlight illuminated a gray fox—our native fox—standing on a little knoll, back stiff and legs spread, muzzle raised to the sky. Fully exposed in my spotlight, he let loose the murderous sound twice more before turning casually and walking away—perhaps even a little disgruntled.

It turns out that it was mating season, and I was—for the second time—the spoiler of a tryst.

As if a nine-year-old girl being strangled in the remote Georgia mountains wasn't dramatic enough, on another night came the deep-chested cries of a two-hundred-pound opera diva being burned alive at the stake some hundred yards away.

Again, you have to take my word for this. That's exactly what it sounded like. The echoes of *this* horrific murder scene stuck with me even more hauntingly than the previous one, simply by virtue of its volume. That poor woman's scream must have paralyzed every creature in the woods for a mile around. Surely, nothing living slept that night.

Before tipi-life, I'd been camping off and on for thirty years, but I had never experienced anything like these sounds. Never. It felt like an improbable statistic. But this offers a perfect testament to the difference between visiting the wild and living in it.

Now that I had become a part of the forest, living in a tipi had graduated me to a school of higher learning. I was in class every hour. If one of these rare sounds erupted within earshot in the forest—just once in the two years that I was there—then I was going to hear it. And so I did.

Though I tried, I was never able to personally witness the second animal. I described the night-rending cry to several biologists, each of whom concurred that I had eavesdropped on the mating call of a mountain lion. Years had passed since the last big cat sighting in my area. To my knowledge, no one in the county even knew that cougars still populated the area. In my heart, my property value skyrocketed—but I kept the information to myself. As much as I loved imagining that big, tawny cat moving through places familiar to me, someone else would covet its company stuffed and mounted in his trophy den alongside the glassy-eyed deer hanging on his wall.

~ 22 ~

Return of the Hunter

Deep in my bones, I loved it. I was stalking a bear—bow in hand, the arrow nocked and held fast to the shelf by my left index finger as I crept along at the speed of smoke drifting on a windless day. Only twenty yards away, the black bear had no clue that I was there. I was hunting again.

It was one on one, just the bear and me. My students had left. I had all the time in the world. Because one of the adults from my class hadn't hoisted the garbage container properly the night before, the bear had reached up, pulled it down, and sunk his teeth into the plastic bin, leaving a series of unforgettable dental impressions. Twenty years later, my young students still gawk at the puncture holes and ask with their eyes the question they do not want to hear answered: *What did that?*

With the trash now properly hung in the trees, the bear snuffled the dirt, looking for food around the circle of stump seats at the base camp. He wasn't going to find anything. My students knew the importance of not dropping crumbs—and here was hungry proof.

"The worst thing you can do to a wild animal is take away its wildness." If nothing else, my students carried that dictum with them from their time with me because they heard it at every meal. After they left, I policed the area just in case. A bear that successfully scavenged here at the fringe of civilization would penetrate deeper into the domain of humans for more sumptuous treats. That path would lead it to its death. My nearest neighbor didn't admire bears as much as I did.

My students knew that bears lived out here. We saw their signs all the time, especially in spring when the famished animals returned to the flow of life after their long winter's sleep. Big rocks lay toppled from their depressions where an ursine tongue had lapped up ant larvae. Giant logs lay stripped of their bark and rotted wood for a feast of beetle larvae. We came across sets of huge footprints in the ferns or in the moist soil by the creek—sometimes so distinct as to show the five formidable claws.

To be a good tracker you have to practice the art of imagining what is not before you at the moment—but recently was. Filling up a visible, definitve footprint with an eidetic picture of an animal's foot, then extending that image up the leg to encompass the entire body of the animal, goes a long way in figuring out where that next track lies. With an imagination so vivid, when you pass your hand through the space that the animal's body had occupied, you realize that only time separates your fingertips and its coat. The air hums with the creature's recent passage. The place crystallizes in your memory forever. You will never pass that spot again without looking for signs of a bear . . . or a bear itself!

As I slipped undetected through the foliage toward this bear in my campground, the air might have crackled with tension, but I had trained myself to keep the adrenaline flow low. Within fifteen yards, the scene could have become electric. I concentrated on keeping calm, confident, and under control. Besides pheromones, science suggests that electromagnetic waves also radiate nervousness from the body. *Be calm. Become like the bear. This is my place, too. We share it. We are the same. I belong here as much as he.* In this frame of mind, I raised my bow in slow motion, drawing smoothly as I did, focusing on the tiniest visible tuft of hair where I would shoot the interloper.

It is at this point—just before the moment of truth—that other hunters say they have lapsed into involuntarily thoughts of what bears are capable of doing to a human. Most accounts repeated or put into print about bears are the horror stories. In the Southeast, the black bear has a reputation for interrupting picnics, but this happens only where he has learned that people are sloppy, illogical, or idiots—which they are when they toss food out of a car, roll up the window, then press their faces to the glass to watch a bear rhapsodize over a potato chip. The moment that bears lose their fear of people, problems arise.

This bear was not a grizzly; but, still, black bears in the wild are not to be taken lightly, just as strangers at your door are to be scrutinized before allowing entry. But bears have a good record with me, perhaps because I spend my woods time in the wilderness rather than in public campgrounds. Every time I have encountered a black bear, without fail it turns and runs from the two-legged devil that has entered its domain.

But move out of remoteness, and the story changes. In the picnic areas of the Smoky Mountains and on the much-traveled Appalachian Trail, black bears have displayed some ingenuity and even aggression. Backpackers careless with their supplies have inadvertently taught bears that people haul delicious food into the forest on their backs. After the bears learned to raid ill-conceived food caches at night, they adopted a bolder ploy that literally cut to the chase: Wait in ambush and charge a hiker head-on as he appears around the bend of the trail. Panicked, the hiker will drop his backpack to make a faster escape, and the bear will have scared the Cheese Whiz out of him.

Then the bear sits down to his meal and runs through his checklist of newly gained knowledge of zippers, snaps, buckles, tie-ropes, Velcro, and bungee cords. If that menu of expertise fails, the bear simply rips apart his "room service" package that was so thoughtfully delivered by the human, who is still sprinting to his car with a whopper of a story to tell.

But what if the hiker doesn't budge? What if he faces down the bear Davy Crockett–style? In every instance that I've heard, the black bear feinted another attack but eventually sulked away.

But there are no rules to the game. Others haven't always been so lucky. Don't let me or anyone else fool you into thinking you can predict what a wild animal will do. Black bears have killed people—even dragged them out of their tents to do it if the literature is correct. In the Boundary Waters of Minnesota and Canada, one bear rushed out into a lake and tried to drown a man. Sometimes the rationale for such attacks is not at all clear to us. That Minnesota bear that attempted to hold a man under water was later put down and, upon an autopsy, found to have a complete stoppage in its gut, which had driven it crazy. The blocking material was a plastic garbage bag. Imagine death by constipation. That could drive anyone to madness.

Experts in the field of bear aggression tell us: If a grizzly attacks, play dead. If a black bear attacks, fight like hell. So there I was holding at full-draw, taking a bead on a black bear's butt within a stone's throw of my tipi. Kids always asked what I would do if a bear pushed through my doorway one night—or worse, through their tent flaps. I always laughed and told them that bears around here would be too afraid to do that. They were wild, not picnic bears.

But as my eye bore down on him over my arrow shaft that day, the bear turned. Peripherally, I spotted an unexpected dash of color on its head: a bright red plastic tag pegged into one ear. Somebody had tagged this bear, probably captured in another area and transplanted here.

Question: What kind of bears are tagged and transplanted?

Answer: Problem bears.

By stalking this bear, I was doing the best thing possible for my camp, for my students, and especially for the bear. The previous night I had made a special arrow just for him. Crowning its point was a hard, blunt, rubber bludgeon tip that, when dispatched by a sixty-pound bow, would pack a shocking wallop but do no permanent damage. The bruise would be temporary; hopefully the lesson would last.

The big muscles in its haunches seemed like the most charitable target, so that's where I shot him. In the moment after impact, I yelled for all I was worth so the bear understood that his tormentor was the dreaded *Homo sagittarius*.

The lumbering creature instantly became a dolphin, springing upward and half-twisting around for a glimpse at his attacker. At this same moment, I ran into the clearing, jumping as high as I could, yelling and waving my bow. If only someone had happened upon us just then. It would have looked like a scene from *Dances with Bears*. My garbage raider charged off into the woods like a boulder gaining speed while crashing down a hillside. Nothing was going to stop him.

In this mountain country of the South, if a hunter kills a bear, he usually gets his picture in the local newspaper along with a line or two about the circumstance of the kill, the weight and size of the bear, and the weapon used. The photos all look pretty much the same: a man and his kill, one smiling, the other . . . not.

If that big furry fellow nosing the leaves before me had wandered up to the closest house, his fate would have been sealed. The man who lives there owns more guns than there are volumes of the Peterson Field Guides.

I hunted for many years, but in time I needed to stop. I don't presume that need for everyone else. I'm not anti-hunter. I am, however, against the way many hunters do hunt—scenarios that include peer pressure, beer, irreverence, and braggadocio. Not everybody, mind you, but many. The quest for a dead bear eludes me. I just don't get it. Does anyone actually crave bear meat? Chipmunk tastes much less oily, less gamey, and you may not think so, but stalking a chipmunk is fifty times harder than stalking a bear without even taking into consideration the difference in target size. I've yet to see the chipmunk/hunter photo in my hometown paper.

The tagged bear never returned. Every year or two another bear showed up, though, and I pulled out the infamous Butt-Knocker Arrow (the official moniker of that legendary projectile). The children and adults who camp at Medicine Bow still love to see that arrow and hear its stories around the campfire, partly for the thrill of imagining a bear in camp and partly for the novelty of considering a grown man skulking around the woods and shooting a bear in the rear with a rubber-tipped arrow. I also like to think that it's reassuring for them to know that the wild things remain wild. Which means, however counterintuitively, that they, the campers, are safer.

At first glance, there doesn't seem to be a simple correlation to this wildness theory for the human animal. The more refined and edified we become through the sciences and arts, the less likely we are to be violent with one another—with a few notable exceptions of course. And if we're not too crowded, that is. Packed together like lab rats, we learn to fabricate a psychological façade of aloofness so that we can distance ourselves emotionally from our neighbors.

Two farmers who drive past each other on a country road are likely to wave. Commuters in city traffic often convey less friendly messages with their hands. In the city we push back nature and overtly spoil the nest. By moving from a daily discourse with the real world, no longer understanding where our water, heat, air-conditioning, or food comes from, we disconnect from our own innate logic, as if the synapses in the brain are widening so that the spark can't jump the gap. We approach chaos.

Never once did I enter my tipi, prepare a meal in my saucepan, then kneel down to an unlighted fire pit and say, "Oops! I forgot to build my fire." But years before, in a house during a power blackout, I repeatedly flipped the same dead light-switch each time I entered the bathroom. I must have done it ten times. What's the difference? Being connected versus being complacent.

When I gathered food from the wild, I knew precisely what I was eating, where it came from, and how fresh and clean it was. Cattails, sochani greens, Indian cucumber root, Solomon's seal tubers, wapato, yellow jacket larvae, acorns, grass seeds, crayfish, groundnut, pine inner bark noodles, and more. When the menu was not wild, my students and I sometimes sat around the campfire enjoying the evening meal we had put together from their store-bought foods, trying to define every ingredient going into our mouths. In one recipe called "El El Bean"—a Mexican dish—I told them that rice is a grass not unlike the grass in the meadow. They eyed me suspiciously. Have you ever seen raw rice outside of a bag?

Every time I visit a school—elementary or high school—and ask the students where electricity comes from, always the same two replies never fail to materialize: lightning and the ocean! Then I ask when they last touched the tissue of a tree. They pause in their note-taking, ponder and calculate, each of their hands resting upon a piece of paper.

Maybe the simplest episodes of our youth will save us. One evening at summer camp, some of the children donned swimsuits and were scooping bucketfuls of clean water from the creek, hauling the water onto the floodplain to bathe with soap. They carefully dipped their buckets and carefully crossed over a log so as not to muddy the water. It all made perfect sense: No one wants to bathe in dirty water.

The Cherokee drank from this creek centuries ago, but there aren't many places where you can sip from surface water any more. If the pre-Columbian Cherokee could travel through time and see the incredible changes wrought upon their land—sprawling cities, massive bridges and highways, behemoth malls, belching factories, shrieking airplanes—their eyes would linger most sadly on the creeks and rivers, seeing what we have done to them in such a short time. Above all other transgressions, this one defilement would reach most deeply into their souls and break their hearts.

As the bathing campers went for another bucket of clear water, a boy named Paul came sloshing down the creek from upstream. He clopped through the water in aquatic oblivion, probably looking for crayfish. When the stirred-up silt reached the bathwater pool, each of the bathers' heads turned upstream in unison, their faces all etched with the same scowl.

Their voices merged like a Greek chorus into a stab of sarcasm. "Thanks a *lot*, Paul!"

Would this brief incident survive their immersion into adulthood and blossom as a global concept that would affect their decisions in their jobs? Some of my first campers are now in their fifties. Every now and then I hear from them—just a few from the early days—and they remind me that such optimism is well-founded. They *do* remember. They have maintained a tie to the real world. A few is something, and there are probably others.

I never said a word to Paul or the bathers. The lesson was complete.

Epilogue

FINAL NIGHT

My home is a house now—full of straight lines, corners, and right angles. Water runs hot from the shower, and the wood heater lasts all day if I stoke it properly. Which I do. I have had lots of practice.

A telephone breaks the silence occasionally, but on the other end of the line usually comes the voice of a friend or a prospective student who may become a friend. Stairs lead to doors, walls frame windows, and the roof lets in not a single drop of rain. I never have to get out of bed in the middle of the night to guide a raindrop down the wall with my finger. There are no skunks under the bed, no snakes upon the shelves. A refrigerator hums in the kitchen with its cornucopia of ready delights. Inside any room I choose, I can create light with the flick of a finger. The bathroom is warm and handy—though not really as handy as a retired mayonnaise jar.

I understand all these conveniences. My experiences have granted me the arcane privilege of living across centuries to witness the evolution of technologies that have delivered our culture to this comfortable point in time. My adventures have led me across several time zones of history in a single lifetime.

Elly lived to see the pouring of the concrete slab upon which the house now sits. Somehow it seems fitting that she didn't witness the raising of the house. She was a tipi-dog. Well, a behind-the-tipi dog.

Teresa, the friend who had called me all those years ago to tell me that my house had burned down, became my wife. She and I were married in front of the tipi under the hemlocks before a small gathering of friends. I made an arrow for the occasion, and as part of the ceremony, I stepped aside with her and explained the symbolism of the paintings on the arrow shaft.

They represented the past and the future, courage and partnership. She liked the substance of it and spoke about the symbols as they applied to her. Then I shot the arrow deep into the woods through an opening in the trees. Later we would look for the arrow together and build a circle of stones where it had landed—a shrine to communication, to our longevity, a place in which to stand and talk of things needful and true. It was to be an eternal nest for the honesty that I wanted to bind us together. That was my greatest hope, for us and any other two who would join their lives together.

When we stepped back to face the semicircle of friends, each guest stepped forward one by one and bestowed us with a gift. No toasters, no silverware, nothing purchased. We had asked friends to bring only natural objects to be left outside at the ceremony site. Most of it rested at the foot of a new hemlock tree that we planted. Some gifts hung in its branches. It looked a little like a Christmas tree.

Someone brought a medicine bundle. Another gave a thin cross-section of cypress that looked like a maze of Celtic crosses. There were feathers, colorful rocks, simple things. On that day, the tree was exactly as tall as I. Today its tapered, feathery crown soars high above me.

Elly gave me away, so to speak, watching the ceremony with the quiet patience of one who knew of her coming end.

After everyone had stepped forward and left a gift, by some unspoken, spontaneous notion, they formed a circle around us. In that moment of unplanned silence, we all listened to the wind in the forest. The January woods around the tipi stood in winter's slumber, and the sun broke through the trees in spears of light. Elly stepped from the crowd and walked toward me, bisecting the circle. Everyone watched her slow progress across the leaves. She had been sick for more than a month with mountain fever, contracted from a tick bite. Her body had become so light that whenever I lifted her she felt hollow. The vet said that she would not recover. She was fourteen years old, ninety-eight if the conversion formula is right.

She labored toward me, moving one leg at a time, breathing with pronounced effort. When she reached me, I was kneeling. She licked my face as I laid my hands on either side of her neck. My face wet and cool from her tongue, I wished that I could always wear that bright patina of her unconditional love on my skin. My life was immeasurably richer for knowing her those fourteen years. She had done it all with me.

I didn't know exactly how soon she would go, but, looking back at the wedding day, it's hard not to believe that she was wishing me well, saying good-bye, leaving me, hopefully, in good hands.

When Elly died, I buried her beneath the small concavity in the ground behind the tipi where she had slept every night that weather permitted. As I dug her grave, I discovered an unusual depression in the earth: a web of roots relaxed into the curve of a hammock. The shovel didn't strike solid ground until almost two feet down. She had slept over an air pocket, an excellent bed that had filled with her body's radiant heat. As I probed the earth, I was still learning from her even after she was gone.

On that night, as I dug the earth beside her, her body shrouded in my favorite shirt, it was easy to imagine her watching me from the other side—just across the metaphorical river. I hoped she was. Besides the good sense of returning our bodies to the earth, another purpose for a grave became evident, one probably practiced since the beginning of human history: to establish a rendezvous place. This function easily comprises half the sanctity of a grave site. I knew I would visit her often, and I was thankful for the defining place.

I planted a young hemlock tree in the depression so that she could become the tree as it grew, the roots absorbing her every molecule. That was more than twenty years ago, and I still miss her every day.

Maybe one day in an electrical storm in a lonely forest, I will kneel to another lost and frightened puppy, and it will rise up to nip my chin just as Elly did when I found her. Maybe she'll even have Elly's look of a coyote-shepherd mix. If she does, I will take her in a heartbeat.

I am still running toward my passions just as I did as a child, running like the wind on a good day, at least symbolically, even running with the deer—though less among them than behind them. My gait is less spry, and the spring in my legs has dwindled.

I was right: The land has shaped me, left its indelible mark. Every herb and tree and shrub is an old friend now.

Hopefully the landscape also touches the very center of the students who visit here to learn the old ways. Sometimes, at the end of a workshop, as adults begin to pack their gear, they stop to tell me so. They talk about a change in themselves from coming to Medicine Bow. With the children, it usually happens years later. They come back as adults when time has given them the insight and vocabulary to verbalize such things.

The tipi stood in the same place for years to come. In time, I replaced it, and then again, each wrapped around the original poles. After I moved into the house, it didn't take long for the conical abode to lose its lived-in look, but that could have changed in a matter of minutes had someone decided to move in. I stayed there off and on as my whims dictated.

Today the lodge is gone. The reflector stone remains—just barely—having crumbled away in layers from years of repeated heating and cooling. It is now too eroded to point at and relate the epic story of hauling it up a mountain. It would sound like a fisherman's tale.

My students and I continued to use the tipi in ceremonies for years. The round space always performed its magic for them. But eventually the material and the poles rotted. Today, I use the original site for special occasions. I speak to students of the ceremony at hand, but it's not the same as when the participants once sneaked looks around the perimeter of the tipi and up into the confluence of its poles. That space is gone, though its memories remain.

In its last years, on those nights when I slept in it out of choice, the flames licked upward again from the fire pit, and the lodge became a lantern. I still stepped back from it, to see it lit up that way. It was a moon rising above the history of all we shared—the tipi, Elly, and I. The moon still illuminates those two years of my life, turns them over for a fresh look. I am reminded of all that I am because of all that I did. I cherish those two winters in a tipi, thankful for every night under that circle of poles, for every call of owl or fox, for every lesson of honesty that only solitude can teach. Part of me—no matter where I sleep—still thinks of turning on one side and reaching out to lay a new stick upon the coals.